Killing Ideas Softly? The Promise and Perils of Creativity in the Classroom

Killing Ideas Softly? The Promise and Perils of Creativity in the Classroom

Ronald A. Beghetto
University of Connecticut

INFORMATION AGE PUBLISHING, INC.
Charlotte, NC • www.infoagepub.com

Library of Congress Cataloging-in-Publication Data

The CIP data for this book can be found on the Library of Congress website (loc.gov).
Paperback: 978-1-62396-364-4
Hardcover: 978-1-62396-365-1
E-Book: 978-1-62396-366-8

CONTENTS

PART III

REALIZING THE CREATIVE POTENTIAL OF THE CLASSROOM

DEDICATION

For my daughter Olivia—May you always find the courage to give voice to your most cherished ideas.

ACKNOWLEDGEMENTS

I thank the editors at Information Age Press for seeing this book through to publication.

Mikhail Bakhtin, the Russian philosopher, described the profound influence that our interactions with other people can have on our own ideas—asserting that our ideas are half ours and half someone else's. I therefore thank my colleagues, students, friends, and family members for the interactions that have influenced my ideas as represented in this book. In particular, I thank James Kaufman and Jonathan Plucker, dear friends and colleagues. Both have had a profound influence on my thinking about creativity. Their influence is clearly evident throughout the pages of this book. I also thank all the prospective and practicing teachers that I have had the privilege to teach. They are a constant source of learning and creative inspiration. I also want to thank all my family members, in particular my wife Jeralynn and daughter Olivia, who provide day-to-day support and acceptance of my own creative ideation. Finally, I thank my colleagues and Dean, Mike Bullis, from the University of Oregon for providing a supportive work environment and granting me a sabbatical so that I could finish this book.

PREFACE

It is the supreme art of the teacher to awaken joy in creative expression and knowledge.

—Albert Einstein

There is little doubt that awakening students' joy in creative expression and learning is one of the most fulfilling aspects of the art of teaching. Doing so, however, is easier said than done. This is because creativity and learning have a strained relationship in schools and classrooms. Indeed, recognizing the value of cultivating children's creativity is one thing; understanding how to meaningfully incorporate it into the everyday classroom is quite another. Fortunately, there is no shortage of insights or suggestions for how teachers might incorporate creativity into the curriculum.

Wading through these suggestions can, however, be quite daunting. This is because there are so many different and sometimes conflicting suggestions. One way to make this process more manageable is to recognize that many of these suggestions can be reduced into one of three different lines of thought.

The first line of thought, what might be called the "radical change" perspective, asserts that including creativity in the classroom requires rethink-

Killing Ideas Softly? The Promise and Perils of Creativity in the Classroom, pages xi–xiii.
Copyright © 2013 by Information Age Publishing
All rights of reproduction in any form reserved.

ing the very nature and goals of K–12 schooling. Proponents of this line of thought would recommend making radical changes to the way teachers teach. The second line of thought represents an "additive change" perspective. Proponents of this view believe that creativity can be included in the existing curriculum, but doing so would require the addition of arts-based activities, the development of new curricular programs, or adopting existing creativity enhancement curricula. In short, proponents of the second perspective ask teachers to add something new to their existing curriculum. Finally, the third line of thought represents a "sight change" perspective. Proponents of this view recognize that creativity can coexist with teachers' existing instructional approach and curricula. The recommendations from proponents of this perspective would focus on how teachers can incorporate creativity into their curriculum by making slight changes to what they already do.

The suggestions and insights that I offer in this book fall into the third line of thinking, the "slight change" perspective. Although recommendations from the first two lines of thought can result in new opportunities for creative teaching and learning, what message do such recommendations send to teachers who are ultimately responsible for teaching traditional academic subject matter? Is it fair to ask teachers to somehow radically change how and what they are required to teach? Can we really expect teachers to include additional creative or arts-based curricula into an already overwhelming set of curricular responsibilities?

I am convinced that slight, manageable changes—made at the informed, professional discretion of teachers themselves—are the best way to see real progress with respect to creativity in the classroom. I simply do not believe that asking teachers to make radical curricular changes or somehow add additional curricula to their existing curricular responsibilities is feasible or reasonable.

The goal of this book, therefore, is to demonstrate that incorporating creativity into one's classroom does not require teachers to give up their academic teaching responsibilities or radically change what they are already doing. Rather, teaching for creativity requires that teachers develop an understanding of the role of creativity in the classroom, common challenges that get in the way of including creativity in one's classroom, and practical insights for addressing those challenges in the context of one's everyday teaching.

To accomplish this goal, I have organized the book into three interrelated sections with three chapters included in each section. Part I focuses on the promise of creativity in the classroom. The three chapters included in Part I involve helping teachers develop their understanding of creativity (Chapter 1); how to recognize and capitalize on easy to miss opportunities to support creativity (Chapter 2); and the connection between creativity and academic learning (Chapter 3).

Part II of the book highlights the sometimes hidden perils of schooling that can undermine student and teacher creativity. The three chapters included in Part II have the aims of helping teachers understand how common instructional beliefs and practices can result in the inadvertent suppression of student creativity (Chapter 4); recognize creativity stifling patterns of classroom talk that teachers sometimes inherit from their own prior schooling experiences (Chapter 5); and understand more serious forms of creativity suppression that can result from a particular type of negative evaluative feedback (Chapter 6).

The final section of the book, Part III, focuses on practical insights and strategies to help teachers incorporate creativity into their everyday curriculum. The three chapters included in Part III have the goals of helping teachers recognize how to establish creativity-supportive classroom environments (Chapter 7); how to incorporate creativity into their lesson planning, instructional activities, and assessments (Chapter 8); and how to be mindful of creativity by providing a summary of reminders and resources (Chapter 9).

Although the primary audience for this book is K–12 teachers, many other audiences interested in creativity (including parents, administrators, prospective teachers, teacher educators, college level teachers, graduate students, and creativity researchers) may also find this book to be a useful introduction to the nature of classroom creativity. In particular, this book will introduce readers to several unexpected opportunities and challenges that teachers face as they attempt to teach for and with creativity.

Developing a more nuanced understanding of creativity is a necessary first step for teachers who want to incorporate creativity into their everyday teaching and to support creativity in the learning and lives of their students. It is my hope that this book will serve as a useful resource for readers interested in learning how to meaningfully include creativity into the everyday classroom. In this way, teachers will be in a better position to actualize the supreme art of teaching: awakening the joy of creative expression in their students' learning and in their own teaching.

PART I

THE PROMISE OF CREATIVITY IN THE CLASSROOM

CHAPTER 1

WHAT IS CREATIVITY?

Creativity is more than just being different.
> —Charles Mingus (cited in Besemer & Treffinger, 1981)

If you were to ask a random group of people what they think of when they hear the word "creativity," you likely would get a range of responses. I would wager, however, that you would also notice some patterns and paradoxes in what you hear. It is likely, for instance, that some people would say creativity has something to do with the arts (e.g., artistic accomplishment, music, poetry), whereas others might mention creativity in the sciences (e.g., describing the process of scientific discovery) or technology (e.g., the development of the microchip or the *iPhone*). You would likely also hear creativity described as some form of unconstrained expression—breaking barriers and constraints, going beyond existing boundaries, and, of course, "thinking outside of the box." Some people would view themselves (and most everyone else) as creative, whereas others would not—believing that "true creativity" is limited to a select few.

Killing Ideas Softly? The Promise and Perils of Creativity in the Classroom, pages 3–16.

You may also find that some people believe that creative ideas just appear, whereas others would argue that creative ideas come from many years of deliberate effort. Some people would associate creativity with the playfulness of children, while others would describe it as being represented only in the highest forms of human accomplishment. A few might mention a dark side of creativity, linking it with some form of deviance or mental illness and providing examples of the tortured and even suicidal artist. Many likely would define creativity as simply an expression of originality, whereas others might explain that it is so complex and mysterious that no words could adequately define it.

Can creativity really be so many of these things—playful and profoundly serious? Most easily identified in the awe-inspiring works of the rare geniuses, yet found in the play of children? Associated with the arts but also expressed in the sciences? Linked with the most profoundly beautiful forms of human expression, yet seemingly overshadowed by a dark side of deviance and mental illness? One way to address these questions is to turn to the scholarly literature and examine how scholars have defined creativity. Doing so might help clarify what creativity means and the role it might play in schools and classrooms.

Several years ago Jonathan Plucker, Gail Dow and I explored what scholars mean by creativity (Plucker, Beghetto & Dow, 2004). Specifically, we wanted to assess how and to what extent creativity was defined in the scholarly literature. We examined the use of the term "creativity" in a sample of 90 peer-reviewed articles. To help ensure that we were examining articles that were focused on creativity, we selected articles only if the term "creativity" was used in the title. We found that of the 90 selected articles, only 38% actually provided an explicit definition of the term and 21% provided no definition. In articles that never provided a definition of the term, authors mentioned *creativity* an average of 32 times—two articles used the term over 100 times without defining it.

These findings suggest that the term creativity is frequently used without being defined—even in scholarly articles that focus on creativity. It is no wonder, then, that creativity has come to mean so many things to so many people. When a concept is used without being defined, it can be used to mean just about anything. If scholarly articles fail to define creativity, then looking to them for a source of information about the nature of creativity may prove to be of little help. But what about when creativity *is* defined? Are there common definitional attributes that might provide helpful insights into the nature of creativity and its role in schools and classrooms?

UNDERSTANDING THE NATURE OF CREATIVITY

Most researchers in the field of creativity studies generally agree on two definitional attributes of creativity: *originality* and *task appropriateness*. In addition to originality and task-appropriateness, creativity researchers often note that creativity is defined within a particular socio-cultural-historical context (Kaufman & Beghetto, 2009; Plucker et al., 2004; Sawyer, 2012).

A good working definition for creativity, then, is simply: *anything that is determined to be both original and task-appropriate as defined within a particular context.* As such, in order to make a determination about whether something or someone is creative, one must also have an understanding of what is meant by originality, the task constraints placed on that originality, and the role that context plays. Each will be discussed in the sections that follow.

Understanding Originality

Originality is the most easily recognized attribute of creativity. In fact, originality or novelty is often viewed as synonymous with creativity (just check any thesaurus). In order for something to be considered creative, it must be considered new, fresh, unique, or unexpected. In a classroom context, for example, a student's sonnet would be considered creative only if it included some new, unique, or original content. This may seem somewhat obvious. What is not so obvious, however, is that originality is not sufficient for creativity.

Creativity researchers have long made distinctions between originality and creativity (Barron, 1955; Guilford, 1959; Maltzman, 1960), yet many people simply equate the two. One reason why we sometimes equate originality with creativity is that the originality of a creative contribution is often more salient or easier to initially recognize than the task-appropriateness or fit of that contribution.

In a study exploring judgments of originality and appropriateness as predictors of creativity, researchers found that originality (as compared to appropriateness) was the most important factor in ratings of creativity (Runco & Charles, 1993). Plucker et al. (2004) found a similar pattern. Specifically, when creativity was defined, uniqueness was the most frequently found attribute, sometimes appearing without mention of usefulness or fit. When fit or usefulness was mentioned, it was always accompanied by uniqueness or novelty. Originality, therefore, seems to be the most obvious attribute when people are attempting to define or make determinations about creativity.

Another reason why we may be inclined to notice originality is that novel or unexpected events present us with opportunities to learn (National Research Council [NRC], 2000). Epicurean learning is an example. We develop our palate by experiencing and attending to unexpected tastes and textures. Language learning is another example. Infants learning to speak learn language by attending to the introduction of new phonemic sounds and patterns. Our ability to attend to novel events seems to be a hardwired survival instinct. Indeed, the survival of our distant ancestors may have hinged on being alerted by unexpected signs of danger (e.g., an unexpected, low growling sound in the dark of night). This alertness to the unexpected can be seen in the behavior of infants, who can be observed attending to novel experiences and events in their environments (NRC, 2000).

Renee Baillargeon and her colleagues have, for instance, demonstrated this tendency in a series of experiments (e.g., Baillargeon, Needham, & DeVos, 1992; Needham & Baillargeon, 1993). These researchers devised scenes and situations whereby they could test infants' reactions to expected and unexpected events. They then observed infants as these events unfolded. An example of an expected event involved showing infants a box that maintained its position when supported, but fell when not supported. An example of an unexpected event was a box that appeared to float in mid-air (when it should have fallen). The researchers found that unexpected events held infants' attention reliably longer than did expected events. These results suggest that our ability to attend to unexpected events may be a hard-wired trait (NRC, 2000).

Of course we don't always notice unexpected events. There are situations when we fail to see even the most surprising of events—a phenomenon that psychologists have called *inattentional blindness* (Mack & Rock, 1998). Researchers have consistently demonstrated that people fail to see a range of unexpected stimuli when focused on some other aspect of their environment (Neisser, 1979; Simons & Chabris, 1999). In a series of studies exploring this phenomenon, researchers had participants observe a brief video clip of a small group of people passing basketballs to each other. The participants were asked to focus on counting the number of passes made by a particular subset of the group. A few moments into the clip, a person—in some cases a woman with an open umbrella (Neisser, 1979), and in other cases a person in a gorilla suit (Simons & Chabris, 1999)—walks (or in the case of the gorilla, dances) in a direct path through the center of the scene and exits. Invariably, some observers fail to see this surprising event and are incredulous that they would miss something as blatantly obvious as a woman with an open umbrella or a dancing gorilla!

With respect to creative expression in the classroom, students' creative ideas during the course of routine class discussions and assignments serve as the unexpected events and sometimes suffer the same fate: being missed or overlooked by their teachers (Beghetto, in 2013a). This form of inattentional blindness, as will be discussed in Chapter 2, occurs in the fleeting moments of the classroom when creative ideas, if attended to, would present teachers with important opportunities to develop students' creative potential.

Inattentional blindness aside, our propensity to attend to novelty may sometimes get in our way of recognizing that creativity also requires appropriateness and fit. This is problematic both from the perspective of the creative observer and the creative actor. With respect to the creative observer, if we fail to recognize that creativity also requires appropriateness, we can end up equating negative forms of deviance with creativity (Feist, 1998; Plucker et al., 2004). With respect to the creative actor, there is also danger in viewing creativity as a form of unconstrained originality. As Professor Mark Runco has explained, "the danger is that an individual can forget that there is a distinction between reality in the environment and reality in one's own thoughts" (2003, p. 30).

Consider, for instance, the outlandish, often dangerous, and sometimes deadly enactment of unusual ideas that earn widespread notoriety in *YouTube* videos and websites like *Failblog.org*, and *Darwinawards.com*. Clearly, educators do not want to cultivate such blind originality in youngsters. Indeed, in the context of the classroom, encouraging unbounded originality would be a recipe for curricular chaos—creating a host of problems that not only would get in the way of teaching and learning, but also the development of students' creative potential.

When creativity is equated with originality, it is easy to understand how teachers might come to associate creativity with negative forms of deviance (e.g., disruptions, off-task behavior, and curricular chaos) and feel that creativity has no legitimate place in their classrooms (Beghetto & Plucker, 2006). Fortunately, creativity is not simply unbounded originality; rather, creativity is a form of "constrained originality" (Keller & Keller, 1996). Put simply, a creative sonnet contains originality in how the poet uses content, but it is still a sonnet. In this way, creativity contains originality that also fits the task.

The idea that creativity can, and often must, thrive within constraints is rarely recognized in popular conceptions of creativity. One reason is that popular conceptions of creativity often suggest that constraints suppress creativity and should be eliminated. Take a moment to think about common slogans associated with creativity, such as "think outside of the box," "free your mind," and "eliminate all constraints." These slogans sound liberating, but in reality creativity always involves constraints (Sternberg & Kaufman, 2010). Understanding the nature of creativity, therefore, requires understanding constraints.

Understanding Constraints

Constraints provide an important and necessary counterbalance to originality. The results of a recent study (Ward, 2008), for example, demonstrate how originality requires constraints. Participants in the study were instructed to develop ideas for a new sport. The ideas that were most favorably rated (i.e., rated as actually playable) were ideas based on preexisting sports rather than more original, less familiar ideas. These results suggest that more constrained originality is more likely to be viewed as favorable or acceptable than less constrained originality.

Another example is the improvisational creativity of a jazz ensemble. When jazz musicians engage in creative improvisation, they are not making music out of nothing, randomly stringing together discordant notes. Such a conception of improvisation, as Berliner (1994) has explained, is "astonishingly incomplete" (p. 544). Berliner further explains that improvisation requires musicians to have developed a "broad base of musical knowledge, including myriad conventions that contribute to formulating ideas logically, cogently, and expressively" (p. 494).

In this way, creativity is not merely a form of unbridled originality but rather is influenced by a wide array of constraining factors. Jazz musicians are constrained by their experience, musical knowledge, their instruments, the venue, the playing of their band mates, and the conventions of their artistic form. Within these constraints, creative jazz musicians are creating new forms, novel combinations, and original expressions of music. Sometimes a musician's creative contribution is slight, yet still noticeable (like might be heard in a local jazz lounge). Other times, and less often, it can be quite radical, such as the influence of Miles Davis, Ella Fitzgerald, John Coltrane, Billie Holiday, and other legends of jazz.

As the above examples illustrate, the types of constraints placed on creativity can be rigidly fixed or more dynamic. But whatever the case, they are necessary. Indeed, as it has been said elsewhere, "that which is novel but has no use, merit, or significance is simply novel, not creative. Likewise, that which is useful but is not novel, unique, or original is simply useful, not creative" (Plucker & Beghetto, 2004, p. 157). Although understanding that creativity is a form of constrained originality helps to clarify the nature of creativity, a key question remains: How does one best judge whether something or someone is creative?

One way that creativity researchers have approached this question is to suggest that judgments of creativity require some observable product (be it an idea, behavior, or artifact) that can be judged by a panel of experts (Amabile, 1996; Kaufman, Plucker, & Baer, 2008). This makes sense because without an observable product, it would be difficult (if not impossible) to make a determination that something or someone is creative. Indeed, how can something be judged to be creative unless it can be observed? Although this approach makes sense for research purposes or more high stakes judgments of creativity, how might teachers judge their students' creativity in a classroom?

Consider, for example, a fourth grade student's poem. A teacher might, understandably, feel that it would be developmentally inappropriate to compare a child's poem to the poetry of an eminent poet like Emily Dickinson or William Shakespeare and, instead, consider the poem in light of other fourth grade students. Although this is quite reasonable, it raises another important question: If a student's poem is only creative as compared to the poems of his or her classmates, should it really be considered creative? Just how creative does something have to be to be considered creative?

What counts as creative is an important question for teachers and creativity researches alike (Smith & Smith, 2010). Some creativity researchers have resolved the ambiguity surrounding what counts as creativity by focusing on more clear-cut examples of creative accomplishment—creative works that have stood the test of time (e.g., Michelangelo's *David*, Picasso's *Guernica*, Darwin's Notebooks). These highly accomplished works are often studied through the analysis of historical records and biographies of highly accomplished creators (Simonton, 2010). Although such research serves as an important source of knowledge for developing an understanding of the highest levels of creativity, it provides little by way of insights into how classroom teachers should think about their students and their own creativity (Beghetto & Kaufman, 2007).

Fortunately, not all creativity researchers have chosen to focus on highly eminent creators. J. P. Guilford, who is sometimes credited with sparking the growth of the field of creativity studies, noted in his presidential address to the American Psychological Association that creativity should be studied from small to large (Guilford, 1950). Guilford emphasized the importance of studying creativity in school children—highlighting, in particular, the need to clarify the role that creativity plays in everyday learning (Guilford, 1950). Since that time, creativity researchers have developed and used a wide-array of techniques to assess creativity.

Some of the most popular assessment techniques include everything from ratings and checklists completed by oneself, one's peers, or one's teachers and supervisors (Kaufman et al., 2008) to paper and pencil tests (Plucker & Makel, 2010). The Torrance Tests of Creative Thinking (Torrance, 1966) remains as one of the most popular ways that educators and researchers have assessed creative potential. Although such assessments have been helpful for studying creativity and even making placement decisions in educational programs, when it comes to the classroom, several important questions remain (Beghetto & Kaufman, 2007).

Consider, for example, a math student who has a unique and personally meaningful insight for how to solve a particular math problem—should that student's insight be considered creative? Put another way, can an idea be said to be creative if only the person—and no one but the person—recognizes that idea as novel and personally meaningful? When it comes to addressing this question, context matters. As such, whenever one attempts to determine whether something is creative (be it an individual insight or a great work of art), the question that should be asked is not whether that something is creative, but rather, as Plucker et al. (2004) note, creative for whom and in what context?

Understanding Context

In order to understand the importance of context, let us return to the question of whether a person's new and personally meaningful idea should be considered creative, even though that idea is not recognized as creative by someone else. Historically, there have been scholars in the field of creativity studies (e.g., Stein, 1953; Vygotsky, 1967/2004) who have addressed this question by stressing the importance of recognizing the role of one's own inner or subjective context when making judgments about creativity.

In more recent years, creativity researchers have expanded on earlier conceptions and have argued that more personal experiences of creativity are perhaps best thought of as examples of creative potential and, because they are personally meaningful, have value in their own right (Beghetto & Kaufman, 2007; Cohen, 1989; Runco, 1996). In line with this tradition, a new and personally meaningful idea, insight, or experience would be considered creative even if no one but the person who had this idea, insight, or experience recognizes it as creative (Kaufman & Beghetto, 2009; Vygotsky, 1967/2004).

This assertion is not as wild as it might first seem. One reason is that it still conforms to the core definitional attributes of creativity: the combination of novelty and task-appropriateness. The difference is that newness and appropriateness are self-judged rather than judged by some external source. Judgment is made in a subjective context. Of course, just because subjective creativity should still be recognized as creativity does not mean that subjective experiences of creativity should be equated with more objective forms of creative expression (Stein, 1953).

Indeed, anyone who recognizes the creativity in a child's personal insight about how to solve a mathematical problem would likely not consider that child's creativity at the same level as the revolutionary mathematical insights of history's greatest mathematicians. In other words, there are qualitatively different levels of creative magnitude (Beghetto & Kaufman, 2007; Kaufman & Beghetto, 2009), and an important goal for educators is to understand these different levels of creativity. This is because teachers who understand these different levels will be in a better position to support the development of their students' creative potential into more objective forms of creative accomplishment (Beghetto, 2007b).

Understanding Levels of Creative Magnitude

When considering the role of creativity in the classroom, it is useful to differentiate between the more subjective versus objective levels of creative expression. The most common distinction has been between little-c (everyday) and Big-C (legendary) creativity (Kaufman & Beghetto, 2009; Kozbelt, Beghetto, & Runco, 2010). Little-c creativity focuses on the creative experiences and expressions of everyday life (e.g., a particularly original holiday letter that is enjoyed by friends and family). Conversely, Big-C creativity refers to clear-cut examples of creative expression (e.g., the revolutionary contributions of creative geniuses). This distinction is helpful because it allows teachers to recognize that the creative expressions of their students (or themselves) do not have to be on the same scale of legendary creators to still be considered creative.

Although somewhat helpful, the little-c and Big-C distinction still lacks sufficient nuance in describing various forms of creativity and thereby can be too exclusive in some cases and too inclusive in other cases (Kaufman & Beghetto, 2009). Consider, for instance, three cooks. First is an expert chef who makes her living cooking in a local restaurant and teaching occasional cooking classes at the local community college. Next is a cooking hobbyist who dabbles with various cooking techniques and recipes in his free time, cooking elaborate meals for friends and family members, but has a full time career in another field. Last is a middle school student who enjoys learning to cook in her school's culinary class and every time she does, has new and personally meaningful insights about how to combine ingredients, flavors, and textures.

Each of these cooks represents qualitatively different levels of creativity; however, none qualify as Big-C creativity (comparable to the legendary accomplishments of Julia Child or James Beard). According to the typical little-c and Big-C distinction, all the non-eminent examples would be grouped together into the little-c category, thereby obscuring important differences among the various little-c creators (Beghetto & Kaufman, 2007).

In an effort to address this problem, my colleague James Kaufman and I have argued for the use of two additional categories *mini-c* and *Pro-c* creativity (Kaufman & Beghetto, 2009). Mini-c creativity is defined as *any novel and personally meaningful interpretation of experiences, actions, and events* (Beghetto & Kaufman, 2007). The mini-c category also helps differentiate the subjective and objective forms of little-c creativity and makes room for the more personal or subjective forms of creativity (Runco, 1996; Stein, 1953; Vygotsky, 1967/2004). In the cooking example above, the young culinary student's new and personally meaningful insights about how to combine ingredients, textures, and flavors would be an example of mini-c creativity, whereas the culinary hobbyist whose original take on cooking (appreciated by friends and family) would be an example of little-c creativity.

Mini-c creativity also represents the creative insights, ideas, and interpretations that occur any time we learn something new and meaningful. It is thereby an important part of the learning process and helps expand conceptions of learning to more explicitly specify the role of creativity in learning. Examples of how mini-c creativity manifests in the classroom and how creativity is part of academic learning are discussed in Chapter 2 and Chapter 3.

Pro-c creativity represents professional-level expertise in a creative area that has progressed beyond little-c creativity but has not yet attained (and may never attain) the legendary status of Big-C creativity (Kaufman & Beghetto, 2009). The Pro-c category distinguishes the professional-level creators who have not yet attained (or may never attain) eminent status, but who are well beyond little-c creators in knowledge, motivation, and performance.

Returning to the above example of creative cooking, the creative meals prepared by the professional chef who cooks for living and teaches cooking classes would be considered an example of Pro-c creativity, whereas the unique and tasty meals prepared by the cooking hobbyist would be considered an example of little-c creativity. Pro-c creativity, like any form of expertise, requires many years of deliberate practice, with some estimates suggesting upwards to 10 years or 10,000 hours of focused development and experience in the particular creative domain (Ericsson, 1996).

The Four-C model of creativity (Kaufman & Beghetto, 2009) helps illustrate how determinations of creativity can range from the immediate inner eye of the creator (as in the case of a child who discovers a painting technique that is only new and meaningful to him or her) to the future eyes of critics and connoisseurs who stand in judgment of creative contributions that span beyond spatial and temporal boundaries (as was the case with Vincent Van Gogh, whose creativity was not recognized during his own lifetime).

It is also important to note that mini-c creativity is not just for kids; rather mini-c creativity is conceptualized as the starting point of all larger creative manifestations—even those that lead to revolutionary breakthroughs (Kaufman & Beghetto, 2009). The invention of Velcro, for instance, started with a subjective, mini-c insight that George de Minstrel had while removing tenaciously sticky cockleburs from his clothing and his dog's fur. De Minstrel examined the cockleburs under the microscope and noted that they had little claws that latched to the loops of fabric in his clothing. He had the insight, based on this experience, that he could manufacture a synthetic version, which is what we now have in Velcro.

Another example is the mini-c insight that Thomas Keller, the acclaimed chef, had while ordering an ice cream cone at Baskin Robbins. When Keller saw how the ice cream cone was served (i.e., held upright in a chrome frame), he had an insight that led to the way he prepares and serves his now iconic dish: salmon cornets. As Keller has explained, "I immediately visualized a scoop of tartare on a little cone made like a tuile, served in a Lucite frame" (Keller as cited in Steinman, 2010).

In summary, the Four-C model can help clarify the categories of creativity (i.e., mini-c and little-c) that inhere in the everyday teaching and learning of the classroom and are, therefore, most relevant for teachers and students. In addition to understanding different categories of creativity, teachers who understand different levels of creative impact can drawn on that understanding to determine what level of creativity might best be suited for their own classrooms. Different levels of creative impact are discussed in the next section.

Understanding Levels of Creative Impact

Creativity researchers have developed various theories to help differentiate among differing levels of creative impact. The Propulsion Theory of Creative Contributions (Sternberg, Kaufman, & Pretz, 2002) is an example of a particularly useful theory for understanding various types of creative contributions. The theory outlines eight different types of creative contributions, ranging from those that represent modifications and advances in a particular domain (through *replication, redefinition, forward incrementation,* and *advance forward incrementation*) to those that attempt to redefine and transform a domain (through *redirection, reconstruction/redirection, reinitiation,* and *synthesis*). Of these types of creativity, *forward incrementation* is typically the most widely accepted because it moves a field forward in a direction it is already headed and does not pose too great a threat to anyone (Sternberg & Kaufman, 2010).

Insights from this theory can be adapted to help teachers think about creativity in a classroom context and provide some guidelines for incorporating and assessing creativity in academic activities and assignments (see also Chapter 8). Moreover, viewing the propulsion theory through the lens of the classroom can help illustrate how most teachers already require some level of creative expression in the projects, tasks, and homework they assign to students.

Consider, for example, the typical science-fair project. Most science teachers would not accept a project that was simply a direct copy of the project they already demonstrated to the class. They also would not accept a student's direct copy of a friend's or sibling's project from last year. Copying is often considered cheating, and teachers frequently instruct students to do their own work, come up with their own ideas, and put things in their own words. In short, teachers request originality, at least in the most literal sense of the word. Similarly, most science teachers wouldn't accept a sonnet about bean sprouts as a substitute for a science fair project. Although a sonnet about bean sprouts might be highly original, it doesn't meet the criteria of scientific inquiry.

As the above examples illustrate, teachers (regardless of their subject area) typically are looking for some type of creative contribution from their students, at least at the level of *replication*. Replication is not a direct copy, but rather a slightly new take on an accepted form (Sternberg et al., 2002). In this way creative expression in the classroom can lean more towards the fit criterion (meeting academic subject matter constraints) and less toward the originality criterion (students own, unique twist on an assignment) and still be considered creative. Replication, of course, is not the only form of creative expression that is appropriate for the classroom. Various other levels of creativity from the propulsion model (Sternberg et al., 2002) can also be modified for a classroom context.

Redefinition, for instance, involves looking at an existing perspective from a different point of view. Adapted for a classroom, a social studies teacher could, for example, encourage creative redefinition by asking his or her students to view a historical event from a new perspective—considering both *what* happened and *what if* this happened instead? *Forward incrementation* is a contribution that moves something along in a direction it is already headed (e.g., allowing students to move a class discussion forward by sharing their novel insights and perspectives). *Advance forward incrementation* also takes something forward in the direction it is heading, but does so before others might be ready for it to go in that direction (e.g., a student who is making connections and sharing insights before others have the requisite understanding to see how those connections or insights fit the discussion at hand).

These first four types of creativity (replication, redefinition, forward and advance forward incrementation) are those that can be readily seen in most any classroom on most any day. Moreover, as might be expected, once creative contributions get to the advance forward incrementation level (and beyond), resistance to creative contributions starts to manifest. This is because such contributions are at the level where people are not yet ready, willing, or able to see the relevance. J. S. Bach's contributions are an example. Clerical authorities at Arnstadt reportedly reprimanded Bach for his innovations in how he played the organ (Schrade, 1946), in particular, raising concerns about how he made "many peculiar variations in the chorale... [how he] smuggled many foreign tones into the melodies, and thus greatly confused the congregation" (p. 163). Of course the uniqueness in Bach's style is one of the things that made Bach stand out as a great composer in the eyes of later generations who were willing and able to appreciate the musical relevance in his innovations.

The last four types of contributions in the propulsion model are rare, but still possible in a modified form for the classroom. These contributions can pose significant challenges because they are, by definition, aimed at rejecting and transforming existing conventions and practices. The first is *redirection*, whereby a creative contribution diverges from where something was headed (e.g., a child shares an unexpected insight during class discussion and takes the discussion in a new, unplanned direction).

Next is *reconstruction/redirection*, which pertains to a contribution that moves something back to an earlier state and then takes it in a new direction (e.g., a teacher or student returns to an earlier point in a class discussion and then introduces an idea that takes the discussion into a new, unexpected direction). Then there is *reinitiation*, which refers to a contribution that moves something to a new starting point and moves it forward from there (e.g., a student comes up with a new way of describing something, and the class adopts it as a category and uses it in subsequent discussions and activities). Finally, *synthesis* refers to a contribution that combines existing paradigms into something new and moves forward from that new combination (e.g., a project-based learning activity that combines math, geology, and history learning and instruction in a novel way).

Teachers, ultimately, have to rely on their professional judgment when determining what level of creative contribution is appropriate for a given assignment, task, or situation. However, teachers likely will recognize that they already ask for some level of creativity from their students, and by being aware of different levels and types of creativity, they will be in a better position to determine when it might be appropriate to propel their students' (and their own) creativity beyond the current level.

CONCLUDING THOUGHTS

The goal of this chapter was to help clarify the nature of creativity so that teachers can understand how it might play a role in their classrooms. As was discussed, creativity involves a combination of originality and appropriateness as defined within a particular social-cultural-historical context. These definitional constraints provide necessary boundaries for considering whether and how students' original contributions are task-appropriate and thereby creative. Helping students learn to combine originality with task-appropriateness is an important step teachers can take to nurture students' creative potential and develop their creative competence.

Understanding the role that originality, constraints, and context play in making determinations about creativity can help teachers avoid falling into common stereotypical beliefs and biases surrounding the nature of creativity (e.g., creativity is not for everyone, creativity is too disruptive) and, instead, focus on finding ways to incorporate creativity into their existing learning activities and assignments.

Although identifying opportunities for students to express their own unique perspectives in the context of structured assignments is an important way to support creativity, it is also important for teachers to recognize that creativity also manifests in surprising, unplanned curricular moments of the everyday classroom. As will be discussed in Chapter 2, when it comes to developing a classroom that supports creativity, these unplanned moments are just as important as (and, in some cases, more important than) planned creative activities. By understanding how creative ideation manifests and develops, teachers will be in a better position to nurture (rather than inadvertently suppress) students' creative potential.

CHAPTER 2

CREATIVE MICROMOMENTS

The things that children wonder about, think, and invent are deep and tough.
Learning to hear them is, I think, at the heart of being a teacher.
                                                                —Ball, 1993, p. 374

Creative micromoments are brief, surprising moments of creative potential that emerge in everyday routines, habits, and planned experiences (Beghetto, 2009b; 2013a). Micromoments occur anytime there is a rupture in what is expected or when events take a surprising turn. The surprising, unscripted nature of micromoments opens windows of creative opportunity. In this way, micromoments are defining moments when it comes to recognizing and developing creative potential.

Creative professionals (e.g., artists, musicians, improvisational actors, photographers, scientists) recognize and capitalize on the creative potential of micromoments. They are able to see the creative possibilities that can emerge from going off-script, playing a wrong note, drifting away from the plan, or otherwise entering uncertain territory. They are also able to see the creative potential that inheres in subtle, unexpected events of everyday life.

Claude Monet, the famous impressionist, is an example of someone who capitalized on such moments. Monet embodied the impressionist's ethos

---

Killing Ideas Softly? The Promise and Perils of Creativity in the Classroom, pages 17–30.
17

of exploring the single moment and recognized "the visual freshness of that first fleeting moment, free of categories of perception or traditional precept" (Heinrich, 2000, p. 32). It was Monet's recognition of this potential that resulted in some of his most famous and arresting meditations on events that might otherwise seem mundane. Monet was able to see these moments for what they were: creative opportunities. As Paul Cezanne, a fellow artist, aptly summarized, "He was only an eye—but what an eye!" (cited in Heinrich, 2000, p. 32).

Although Monet seemed to have been blessed with a special eye, viewing life with the *eye of Monet* is not limited to impressionist painters. The eye of Monet can be cultivated and developed in our daily lives and classrooms. In so doing, teachers can be in a better position to recognize and cultivate the creative potential of their students. Prior to considering how such an approach might be developed in the classroom, it may be helpful to consider a few examples of how accomplished professionals approach their work with an eye of Monet.

HOW CREATIVE PROFESSIONALS SEE MICROMOMENT OPPORTUNITIES

Photographers tend to recognize the creative potential that can be found in the brief, passing moments of everyday existence. Man Ray (Emmanuel Radnitzky), the renowned photographer and artist, was an example of someone who incorporated the eye of Monet approach in his professional work. Ray recognized the creative possibilities found in spontaneous, fleeting moments and was able to capture these micromoments in his work. As Ross (1982) has explained, "For Ray, the spontaneous, the fleeting moment, was everything" (p. 4). Photography was, according to Ross, a means of creative exploration for Ray, "never an end in itself" (p. 4).

Another example is professional photographer Bill Lockhart, who has explained that his most successful and creative photographs were those in which he was able to capture brief, naturally occurring moments (e.g., sun light breaking over treetops). As Lockhart (2012) has explained, "after making tens of thousands of photographs...the best were those that captured a specific and fleeting moment of time... this is the beginning, and at the heart of, creativity" (par. 1).

Looking for and capturing specific fleeting moments is one of the most appealing things about photography in general and, not too surprising, became the primary marketing tagline of Kodak camera company: *These are the moments. Kodak moments.* The Kodak tagline speaks to an eye of Monet approach, which highlights the notion that everyday fleeting moments are important. Of course, Kodak is trying to sell cameras. Still, the tagline speaks to the realization of the creative potential that can be found in recognizing and exploring such moments. Approaching one's work and life with the eye of Monet doesn't require the purchase of a Kodak camera, a set of oil paints, or any other special tool. Rather, it simply requires the recognition that such moments can be found in everyday occurrences and a readiness to explore such moments.

This recognition and readiness is a skill that teachers of improvisational comedy attempt to develop in new improvisational players. One of the first techniques that improvisational comedians learn is the "Yes, and" technique (Halpern, Close, & Johnson, 1994). The "Yes, and" technique helps performers welcome and build on surprising ideas, actions, and utterances of their improvisational teammates. For accomplished improvisational performers "Yes, and" is likely more of a habit than a technique—allowing them to pay attention to unexpected moments and explore the creative direction that such moments will take them.

Paying attention to single, brief moments is at the heart of the eye of Monet concept and evidenced in the highly accomplished improvisation of T. J. Jagodowski and David Pasquesi (alumni of the renowned Second City improvisation group). Jagodowski and Pasquesi recognize that the most important skill of improvisation is paying attention to everyday occurrences and requires daily practice (Karpovsky, 2009).

Both Jagodowski and Pasquesi practice this skill prior to their evening performances by simply strolling through the city (together and sometimes alone), paying attention to the people, interactions, and everyday occurrences that naturally play out before them. Then, at the outset of their hour-long improvised comedic performances, they simply pay attention—patiently looking around the auditorium, looking out into the faces of the audience members, and then at each other. They are waiting. Looking for the moment. The process is non-verbal. They do not solicit topics or themes from the audience. They simply watch and wait. Somewhat ironically, then, their first move in their live performance is to not say anything, but rather to stand still, watch, pay attention—waiting for the opportunity to act.

This is because they recognize that the fleeting, beginning moments of their performance are filled with creative possibilities. As Pasquesi has explained, "at the very beginning is when all the information comes out...in a look or a posture, in the very beginning we can explore that for an hour" (Karpovsky, 2009). It may seem quite remarkable that a single, fleeting look—what for most people would be viewed as a throw away moment—could be drawn on and explored for an hour or more. This, however, is a common theme for those who have learned how to approach unexpected micromoments with the eye of Monet.

Monet himself would devote long stretches of time paying attention to and meditating on the micromoments that played out in a particular setting. He would, as Stokes (2001) has reported, sit in a boat, focus on a particular object (e.g., poplars), and create many paintings of that object across various times (dusk, evening, sunset, autumn, spring) and conditions (windy and overcast weather). Monet put himself in the position to observe and capitalize on a surprising micromoment occurrence in what was otherwise a mundane setting.

Even rock-and-roll musicians can (and do) approach their artistry with the eye of Monet. Jack and Meg White, members of the two-person music group White Stripes, are an example. As is typically the case when music groups go on tour, the schedule and venues are established well in advance. The same was true for the 2007 White Stripes tour of the Canadian territories. Importantly, however, the group also built in impromptu day shows—what Jack White called "side shows" (Malloy, 2009). The locations of the impromptu shows included everything from flourmills to bowling alleys.

The unexpected nature of these shows resulted in a break from the normal set and presented fleeting moments of creative expression that could not be replicated. As Jack White has explained, "once you have a moment something beautiful happens—if you go back and try to repeat it, chances of it being beautiful again are almost zero" (Malloy, 2009). Such an approach is risky. One cannot be sure of the outcome, and there are no safety nets of the traditional concert (e.g., sound checks, sold tickets, and well constructed stages). Still, the sideshows offered new possibilities, insights, and opportunities for the two musicians—allowing them to experience something new and unexpected with their music.

The above examples, taken together, are intended to illustrate how approaching micromoment opportunities with the eye of Monet can transform seemingly throw away moments into easily recognizable, unambiguous forms of creative expression. Indeed, the ability of these highly accomplished creators to recognize and respond to micromoment opportunities has resulted in the production of unique and meaningful forms of creative expression.

Cultivating the Eye of Monet

There is both benefit and danger in using highly accomplished creators as examples of people who have cultivated the eye of Monet. The benefit is that such examples provide clear-cut demonstrations of creative expression. The risk is that using such examples may imply that the eye of Monet is an innate trait available only to the elect few. It is true that only a tiny proportion of people actually achieve legendary levels of creative accomplishment (cf., Simonton, 2010). Indeed, taking a set of paints out in a row boat and making 24 portraits of trees or water lilies, if you haven't spent the requisite time learning to paint, has almost zero chance of yielding anything close to a painting comparable to Monet's. Fortunately, cultivating the eye of Monet is not about trying to become the next Monet. Rather, enhancing one's own eye of Monet is something that can be attained. But doing so requires practice and investing the requisite time and effort in developing domain-specific expertise.

The Expert Eye

Cultivating one's own eye of Monet requires putting forth the requisite time and effort to develop of an expert eye. To become an expert typically requires a decade (or more) of intensive preparation (Ericsson, 1996). This intensive preparation and experience allows experts to see things differently as compared to beginners and amateurs—noticing features of situations and problems that go unnoticed by people who are less experienced (NRC, 2000). When expert chess players are presented with challenging chess positions, they are more likely to select better moves compared to less experienced chess players (de Groot, 1965).

Experts also see expressions of creativity differently than do people with less experience. This is why scientific journals use panels of expert raters and why one of the most popular creativity assessment techniques uses expert judges (Amabile, 1996). This technique, called the Consensual Assessment Technique or *CAT* (Amabile, 1996), has been used in numerous studies of creativity. In studies that have compared experts' ratings with the ratings of beginners or amateurs, experts have been found to see creativity differently than novices. In judging the creativity of poems and short stories, for example, researchers have found that experts' ratings tend to differ from novices in how they rate creativity (Kaufman, Baer, Cole, & Sexton, 2008; Kaufman, Baer & Cole, 2009).

With respect to recognizing the potential of creative micromoments, skilled creators have prepared themselves to see and capitalize on opportunities for creative expression. This ability of accomplished creators to see opportunities has been called "problem finding" (Getzels & Ciskszentmihalyi, 1976). Problem finding is different from traditional problem solving because it explains how creators identify problems in the first place and how creators "bring their subjective experience to understand the problem" (Kozbelt et al., 2010, p. 34).

Cultivating an eye of Monet approach in classroom teaching, therefore, requires the experience and expertise necessary to realize and respond to the creative opportunities found in the everyday, unscripted micromoments of the classroom. Awareness of the value of doing so and understanding how other teachers have successfully done so is an important first step toward cultivating this approach in one's own teaching.

SEEING CREATIVITY IN THE
MICROMOMENTS OF THE CLASSROOM

In the classroom context, micromoments occur any time the curriculum takes an unexpected or surprising turn (Beghetto, 2009b). Such moments are present in everything from a student stumbling forth an unexpected idea during a class discussion to an unexpected result emerging from a routine science experiment. Anyone who has ever taught has experienced these surprising, unplanned curricular moments.

Put another way, micromoments occur when the curriculum-as-planned meets the curriculum-as-lived (Aoki, 2004; Beghetto & Kaufman, 2011). This meeting of the *planned* versus *lived* curriculum creates an unexpected curricular occurrence, which can go unnoticed or seem so disruptive that teachers, understandably, want to get back to the lesson plan. Creative teachers, however, view such moments as opportunities for the emergence of creative learning. These moments represent an opening in the curriculum that allows students and teachers to explore, learn, and experience something new, unscripted, and unplanned.

Curriculum theorist Ted Aoki (2004) has described such moments as "a space of generative interplay between the planned and live(d) curriculum...a site wherein the interplay is the creative production of newness, where newness can come into being...an inspirited site of being and becoming" (p. 420). Aoki goes on to explain that he learned how to see the creative potential in the ambiguous space between the planned and lived curriculum as a curricular opportunity (rather than a sign of chaos). Aoki invites teachers to develop their own ability to see the generative potential of these openings and have the courage to linger in these spaces.

Vivian Paley, early childhood educator and author, serves as a model for how teachers can learn to realize the potential of unexpected curricular moments. Paley (2007) describes how she came to develop her own ability to see the passageway that unexpected curricular micromoments presented (i.e., develop her own eye of Monet) and how her willingness to recognize this potential allowed her to linger more and more in these moments.

More specifically, Paley (2007) explains that once she really started paying attention to her students she was able to clearly see learning opportunities that had "more vitality, originality, and wide-open potential than could be found in any lesson plan" (p. 154). Paley goes on to explain that she soon recognized that if she allowed herself to sustain these moments and actually listen to the voices of her children—rather than drown them out with her own voice and planned lesson—creative ideation would pour forth. This, in turn, altered the way she viewed her role as a teacher: "the rules of teaching had changed; I now wanted to hear the answers I could not myself invent... Indeed, the inventions tumbled out as if they simply had been waiting for me to stop talking and begin listening" (Paley, 2007, p. 155).

Approaching students' unique responses and unconventional ideas with an eye of Monet is easier said than done. Teachers may feel like they have less and less freedom to explore the uncertain curricular places where their students' ideas will take them. Indeed, teachers who work in an era of increased accountability, externally mandated curricular standards, and increased use of standardized assessments find themselves attempting to strike the difficult balance between trying to see the potential creative contributions of children and, at the same time, meeting externally mandated curricular standards.

Encouraging students' unconventional ideas, knowing how to respond to those ideas, and all the while teaching students requisite academic subject-matter is incredibly challenging. This is because, as Ball (1993) has explained, "teachers are responsible for helping children acquire standard tools and concepts...the unusual and novel may consequently be out of earshot...even when the teacher *hears* the child, what is [the teacher] supposed to do?" (p. 385). Knowing what to do in the face of the unexpected is, as discussed earlier, something that comes with deliberate practice and experience.

Researchers have documented the importance of teacher experience and academic content knowledge when it comes to flexibly and effectively working with student ideas and unexpected curricular events. In a study of three elementary science teachers, for instance, researchers found that the most experienced and knowledgeable teacher was more capable of eliciting and working with student ideas as compared to an intern teacher, who tended to respond in ways that discouraged students from sharing their own unique ideas (Akerson, Flick, & Lederman, 2000). Similarly, research examining teachers' in-the-moment instructional decision making has demonstrated that more experienced teachers are more likely to recognize emergent curricular opportunities presented by unexpected curricular moments and also are more likely to respond to those opportunities with improvisational flexibility (Borko & Livingston, 1989; Housner & Griffey, 1985; Sawyer, 2011).

Hearing and responding to students' unconventional ideas requires, as Ball (1993) notes, a type of disciplinary subject matter knowledge that extends "beyond the conventional image of [the particular subject area]" (Hawkins cited in Ball, 1993, p. 114). Teaching for creativity in the micromoments, therefore, requires a form of "disciplined improvisation" (Sawyer, 2004) that comes from a blend of structured disciplinary knowledge and in-the-moment improvisational flexibility (Beghetto & Kaufman, 2011). In this way, teachers can make as-needed adjustments to their planned lessons without letting those lessons drift into curricular chaos.

What might this look like in an actual classroom? The examples that follow are intended to illustrate how creative micromoments might manifest in the everyday classroom and how teachers are able to approach these moments with an eye of Monet— skillfully recognizing and responding to the creative potential that inheres in such moments.

Approaching Unexpected Ideas with the Eye of Monet

One of the most common, yet subtle, classroom micromoments—which has implications for the development of students' creative potential—occurs whenever a student shares an unexpected idea (Beghetto, 2009b). Anyone who has ever led a classroom discussion has encountered unexpected student comments. Such comments can run the gamut from apparent confusion to seemingly willful attempts to derail the lesson.

Although unexpected student ideas can signify a wide range of things to teachers, they are also signifiers of creative potential. This is because creative ideas are, by definition, unexpected ideas (Beghetto, 2009b). Of course, an unexpected idea is not necessarily a creative idea. Indeed, in order for an unexpected idea to be creative, it must also be meaningful in the context of the particular class discussion (Chapter 1). The challenge, as most teachers know, is deciding whether it is worth the time to follow an unexpected idea—risking the expenditure of precious class time, not to mention risking the possibility of taking the teacher and the entire class into a swamp of curricular confusion.

Although there are curricular risks involved in exploring unexpected ideas, there are also important benefits. Indeed, it is in these micromoments that teachers can play an instrumental role in helping students develop their mini-c insights into meaningful little-c contributions—propelling the class discussion forward into new and rich territory that can even enhance academic subject matter learning. Moreover, successful creators have the ability to "move from their personally meaningful and novel interpretations (mini-c creativity) to expressions of creativity that are viewed as meaningful and novel to others (little-c creativity)" (Beghetto, 2007b, p. 268).

Unexpected ideas, viewed in this light, can be thought of as a catalyst for developing students' creative potential and deepening their understanding of academic subject matter. However, in order to determine whether an unexpected idea is a creative idea, teachers need to draw out a student's surprising comment to help assess whether and how the idea might be meaningful and thereby creative.

A few examples might help illustrate. Each of the following examples represents an example of a creative micromoment in elementary school math. They serve as particularly good examples of micromoments because people sometimes feel that elementary mathematics has rather clear-cut, teacher-known answers to problems and thereby is one of the most difficult subject areas in which to recognize and cultivate student creativity.

Example 1: Add six back on and get nine

Consider the following example[1] (adapted from Beghetto, 2009b). Imagine a second grade teacher who recently introduced the topic of double column subtraction to her students. After having taught her students the strategy of "borrowing" to solve such problems, she asks the class to explain why 26 − 17 = 9. The teacher might expect students to use the "borrowing" strategy when explaining their answers (e.g., borrow ten from the twenty, add it to six, that makes sixteen, and then take away seven). What if a student (Gary) unexpectedly explains, "I got nine by adding the three back on to six." Such a response would be an example of a micromoment. It is difficult to tell what exactly this unexpected response signifies. Although it is true that three plus six equals nine, it doesn't seem to be an appropriate response in the context of the stated problem (twenty six minus seventeen).

As such the teacher might interpret Gary's comment as signifying that he was not paying attention or misunderstood the question. On the basis of this interpretation, the teacher might, quite understandably, decide to gently redirect Gary's unexpected response, so as not to confuse other students ("Yes, Gary, three plus six equals nine, but that isn't the problem we are trying to solve...why don't you think about it a bit more...while I call on someone else..."). Although such a response might be typical and seemingly legitimate, doing so is actually a form of "soft dismissal" because the teacher isn't taking the time to explore the reasoning behind Gary's unexpected response (see also Chapter 5).

Rather than dismiss or redirect Gary's unexpected idea, the teacher might quickly request an explanation, "Help us understand where the three came from Gary..." This signifies to Gary that his response is not making sense and also provides an opportunity for him to reveal the potentially creative thinking behind his response (Beghetto, 2007b).

An example of the creative thinking that might be revealed when students have the opportunity to explain their unexpected responses is illustrated in an explanation offered by an actual second grade student (presented in Kamii, 2000): *"First you take off 10 from 20 and that would be 10. . .take off 7 more and now you have 3...add the 6 back on and that would be 9."*

As this example illustrates, in the micromoment manifestation of unexpected ideas, creative ideas may be indistinguishable from what otherwise seems like confused or inaccurate ideas. By encouraging students to share their reasoning behind such ideas (rather than simply dismissing them),

---

[1] The initial portion of this example is a hypothetical adaptation from an actual lesson and represents a commonly used strategy for teaching the concept of "borrowing" when subtracting. Importantly, however, the student's explanation in the second portion of the example (i.e., how he arrived at the answer of 9 when subtracting 17 from 26) represents an actual second grade student's explanation (presented in Kamii, 2000).

teachers can uncover otherwise hidden creative insights. In this example, the student's idea is initially unexpected, but his reasoning makes sense and can be thought of as a classroom example of *forward incremental* creative contribution (Sternberg, Kaufman, & Pretz, 2002).

As discussed in Chapter 1, this type of creative contribution is likely to be accepted because it propels, in this case the class discussion, in the direction it was already headed (i.e., how students arrived at the answer "9" when subtracting 17 from 26). Of course, the idea would go nowhere if the teacher didn't have the in-the-moment presence of mind to explore the reasoning behind the unexpected idea.

Classroom based creative contributions that take the form of forward incrementation require teachers to have in-the-moment awareness. Once recognized, teachers are more likely to see their value and accept them as little-c contributions. But what about ideas that are not so easily accepted? Or ideas that may take a class discussion in a direction that the teacher (or other students) may not be ready to take? And how about ideas that redirect a class discussion into a completely unexpected direction? The following examples are intended to help illustrate the kinds of ideas that have the potential to take discussions in directions that the teacher and other students may not be ready to take.

Example 2: Two Plus Two Doesn't Always Equal Four

Imagine the following situation, adapted from Beghetto (2013b), of a first grade teacher who wants to quickly review a few basic math facts prior to introducing a more complex math activity. As part of the review, the teacher asks students to answer the known answer question of: "What does two plus two equal?" Multiple students correctly respond: "four!" Imagine if one student, Sophia, states: "Two plus two doesn't always equal four." Sophia's unexpected response represents a momentary rupture in the curriculum-as-planned. Instead of quickly reviewing math facts as the teacher intended, Sophia introduced a moment of uncertainty. The teacher is now confronted with a two-fold micromoment decision.

The first decision for the teacher is how to respond to such an assertion: Do I spend class time attempting to understand Sophia's unexpected comment or do I quickly correct Sophia—helping her understand the known answer—so as not to waste class time and create additional confusion? A teacher who approaches uncertain moments such as this one with the eye of Monet may recognize that there is potential value in exploring the idea further (e.g., "Okay, Sophia, can you give us an example of when two plus two can equal two?").

Asking Sophia to explain provides an opportunity to recognize the creative potential of Sophia's assertion. Sophia, for instance, might explain,[2] "If you have two hungry cats and two fat mice, you end up with two fed cats." The teacher is now confronted with a secondary decision of whether to follow the new direction presented by this idea (e.g., "Can anyone else think of an instance when two plus two equals something other than four?") or refocus the students back to the planned lesson (e.g., "Yes, Sophia, I suppose that's true. Now, let us return to reviewing our math facts…").

By taking the time to explore a student's unexpected idea, teachers can reveal creative insights that can take a lesson in new and potentially generative directions. Importantly, doing so does not always pay off in the form of meaningful learning. Teachers, ultimately, need to rely on their professional judgment in deciding what to do in such instances. Of course, such decisions are not always easy to make because there are a variety of factors to consider.

Case study research (van Zee, Iwasyk, Kurose, Simpson, & Wild, 2001), for example, has identified various factors and potential pedagogical dilemmas that teachers face when deciding whether to "stay and discuss" an unexpected student utterance or "get through the lesson." These factors include: the intent of the lesson, how interested the other students are in pursuing a new topic, how knowledgeable teachers themselves are about the topic, and how much time is available (van Zee et al., 2001).

Clearly, teachers face a variety of decisions when confronted with unexpected student comments. The next example illustrates the value and challenges that inhere in taking the time to explore and develop students' unexpected ideas into meaningful classroom contributions.

Example 3: Sean's Numbers

This final example is from an actual third grade mathematics lesson (as discussed in Ball, 1993 and Bass, 2005). The teacher (Ball) and her students had been working on odd and even numbers. One day, at the start of class, a student (Sean) stated, somewhat out-of-the-blue, "I was just thinking about six…it could be an odd and an even number" (Bass, 2005, p. 424). Sean's idea that six is a number that can be both "an odd and an even number" is, by most any account, quite unexpected and unconventional. Such a surprising assertion presented the teacher with a micromoment decision, similar to what was discussed in the previous examples. Should the teacher spend class time exploring such an unconventional and seemingly confused idea of an eight-year-old child, or should the teacher gently correct the student so as not to introduce Sean's seemingly confused idea to his 17 classmates?

---

[2] Although this example is hypothetical, it represents a modified version of an actual discussion between a researcher and a group of first grade children (reported in Matusov, 2005).

In this instance, the teacher decided not to directly correct or redirect Sean but instead restated Sean's assertion, tried to help clarify what he was saying, and invited Sean's classmates into the exchange. After some discussion, a student challenged Sean to "prove it to us..." and Sean drew the following example on the board (adapted from Ball, 1993, p. 385):

o o l o o l o o l

Sean explained that, as illustrated in the figure, six is an odd number because it is made up of three groups. Sean also recognized, based on the class's working definition of even, that six could also be even because even numbers can split into two even groups (two groups of three), as illustrated below (adapted from Ball, 1993, p. 385):

o o o l o o o

Sean, based on this logic, had the mini-c insight that six could be both even and odd, whereas a number like five would be only odd (because you can't split it evenly) and four would be only even (because it can only be split evenly in two groups of two). The teacher and students in the class eventually came to understand and see the appropriateness in Sean's idea when describing numbers, coming to call numbers with these special properties, "Sean's numbers." The teacher asked Sean to develop a definition, which he eventually did: "Sean's numbers have an odd number of groups of two" (Ball, 1993, p. 387).

The understanding and acceptance of Sean's numbers, however, did not come easily. Sean's classmates and his teacher had struggled with how Sean's idea might actually fit before they eventually came to recognize it as a unique and meaningful way of thinking about numbers (i.e., a little-c contribution). One of Sean's classmates, Mei, shared her interpretation of what Sean was saying, "I think what he's saying is that you have three groups of two. And three is an odd number so six can be an odd number and an even number" (Bass, 2005, p. 426).

Mei engaged Sean in this discussion, stating that she had difficulty accepting his idea because other numbers, like ten, share the same properties. In so doing, Mei actually helped Sean clarify and expand his mini-c idea, "I didn't think of it that way...thank you for bringing it up" (Bass, 2005, p. 427). This further exasperated Mei because she thought it would eventually lead to all numbers being classified as odd and even. Sean's peers, Mei in particular, had difficulty accepting Sean's unconventional mini-c idea because it prompted the class to go in a direction they were seemingly not ready to go.

Returning to the propulsion model of creative contributions (Sternberg et al., 2002), Sean's idea was beyond the level of *forward incrementation* and could be thought of a form of creative *redirection,* moving the class away from the direction it was currently moving with respect to their understanding of odd and even numbers. As might be expected, such ideas typically face resistance (and even outright rejection).

Indeed, Sean's peers were not the only ones who wrestled with the merit of his mini-c idea. Sean's teacher also struggled with the fit of his idea, at turns wondering and worrying whether accepting this idea would be beneficial to student understanding or create confusion among all of her students (Ball, 1993). Ball found herself having to "grapple with whether or not to validate nonstandard ideas" (p. 387)—worrying that by choosing to accept such ideas she might induce confusion in the classroom and interfere with the more conventional and requisite concepts and understandings that she, as a teacher, was expected to help students learn.

Ultimately, she decided to accept and endorse "Sean's Numbers" in her classroom—reasoning that doing so would introduce her students to learning about how mathematical knowledge evolves through the introduction of novel ideas. As a result, she found that it engendered pride in Sean and interest among her students, and she found no evidence of Sean's numbers interfering with student's conventional learning and understanding of even and odd numbers. Fortunately, rather than simply rejecting Sean's mini-c idea, Sean's teacher provided the time and curricular space necessary to forge his idea in the crucible of classroom discussion—allowing the potential merits of the idea to be more fully explored, elaborated, and eventually recognized as a legitimate little-c creative contribution (i.e., one that was unique and that others recognized as useful with respect to the definition and classification of numbers).

Taken together, these three examples illustrate how exploring student ideas can uncover students' hidden mini-c creative ideation and how such insights can then be developed and expanded into generative little-c ideas. Doing so develops students' creative competence and can also enrich the learning and understanding of peers and teachers. Of course, doing so does not always reveal creative thinking. Still, by drawing out the thinking behind unexpected ideas, teachers can help students become aware of academic subject matter conventions and constraints, teach them how to better articulate the relevance of their ideas in light of those conventions and constraints, or even help them realize that sometimes it is necessary to let go of a particular idea in search of more viable ones (Beghetto, 2007b).

CONCLUDING THOUGHTS

The purpose of this chapter was to highlight the importance of teachers being able to recognize and respond to micromoment opportunities that manifest in the everyday classroom. Taking time to explore students' unexpected ideas should not, however, be interpreted as suggesting that teachers should abandon academic conventions or even more direct forms of instruction.

Recall from Chapter 1 that creativity requires constraints. In the context of the classroom, those constraints pertain to the academic conventions of the particular learning task. The importance of recognizing and responding to micromoments simply means taking time to explore and attempt to understand students' mini-c utterances and then work with students—by drawing on established conventions and strategies—to help them develop their personal interpretations into appropriate subject-matter-specific little-c contributions.

Indeed, a fundamental part of teaching, particularly in subject areas like mathematics, involves helping students learn existing strategies and procedures for arriving at correct answers. The point is, as will be discussed in the chapters that follow, both meaningful learning and students' creative competence can suffer when instructional practices short-circuit the exploration and elaboration of students' mini-c ideas.

The most effective teachers—those who successfully teach for creativity—are able to strike a balance between the direct teaching of existing strategies and procedures *and* the flexibility necessary to provide opportunities to explore and develop students' emerging mini-c understandings (Beghetto & Kaufman, 2011; Beghetto & Plucker, 2006). The challenge facing teachers is, as Sawyer (2011) notes, getting the balance just right. This is where teachers' expertise comes in—having the experience and knowledge necessary to effectively blend necessary structure with in-the-moment improvisations. Creative teaching, therefore, "involves *both* the possession of a large knowledge base of expertise and knowledge of improvisational practice—of how and when to use that knowledge" (Sawyer, 2011, p. 11).

Developing the requisite combination of the knowledge necessary to recognize creative opportunities presented by classroom micromoments and the in-the-moment awareness of how to best respond to such micromoments is a common thread running through the remaining chapters of this book. This knowledge starts with understanding the connection between creativity and academic learning, which is the focus of the next chapter.

CHAPTER 3

THE CONNECTION BETWEEN CREATIVITY AND LEARNING

A creative act is an instance of learning…a comprehensive learning theory must take into account both insight and creative activity.

—Guilford, 1950, p. 446

Life in the 21st century is filled with uncertainty. Rapid technological, social, economic, and global changes contribute to this uncertainty. Although it is not easy to predict what the future might hold, one thing is clear: Students will need to be better equipped to navigate the complex and ill-defined nature of life in the digital age (Wells & Claxton, 2002).

Anna Craft, a UK-based creativity researcher, has argued that life in the digital age has altered the very nature of childhood (Craft, 2011). Youngsters, with the requisite technology, have the unprecedented ability to access information and learn almost anytime or anywhere. In addition to being able to access vast databases of information and engage in digitally mediated learning, students also have new ways to create and contribute their own content (Craft, 2011). As such, the line between teacher and student can easily blur in the digital age.

Killing Ideas Softly? The Promise and Perils of Creativity in the Classroom, pages 31–49.

As just one example, consider Adora Svitak, who has been called, "The World's Youngest Teacher" (Bonk, 2009). When Adora was 11 years old, Curtis Bonk, a professor of instructional systems technology at Indiana University, interviewed her and asked how she uses technology for her online teaching.

Adora explained in her interview with Bonk that technology allowed her to reach a wide range of audiences (from elementary school students to teachers). She was also able to teach about various topics and subject areas (e.g., language arts, social studies) and provide teachers with professional development on the use of technology in their own classrooms. The technology that she used also enabled her to provide timely instructional guidance and feedback to her students (e.g., provide on-screen examples and interact with her students).

Readily available technologies have allowed Adora to transform the traditional roles of student and teacher and facilitated her ability to teach what she knows in a very direct and engaging way. As she explained in her interview with Bonk:

> Technology has made this possible by allowing me to demonstrate the process in an immediate and interactive way. When I teach writing, I type up the writing on my screen and show it to the students, word by word, line by line, while incorporating their ideas into the writing. This approach makes writing not just an educational activity, but also a social one; it allows me to interact with the audience and it allows the audience to interact with me. (Bonk, 2009)

At the time of the interview, Adora had already reached more than 300 classrooms and had been featured on numerous major media outlets for her innovative approaches to teaching and learning (Bonk, 2009). Although Adora might represent somewhat of an anomaly,[1] her example illustrates what is possible in the digital age. Indeed, most anyone with Internet access can rapidly retrieve vast amounts of information, collaborate with others around the world, and easily develop and disseminate their own content.

EDUCATING-FOR-THE-FUTURE PARADOX

How might teachers in more traditional, brick-and-mortar K–12 settings better prepare students for increasingly ill-defined, rapidly changing, and unknown futures? One way to think about this question is to recognize that although life in the digital age presents many new and unknown teaching and learning possibilities, the underlying paradox of teachers attempting to prepare students for an uncertain future is not new.

---

[1] She published her first book, *Flying Fingers*, at age seven. She purportedly reads two to three books a day, has written more than 400 short stories, three books, and dozens of poems (Bonk, 2009).

John Dewey, the eminent philosopher of American education, writing over a century ago noted, "With the advent of democracy and modern industrial conditions, it is impossible to foretell definitely just what civilization will be twenty years from now. Hence it is impossible to prepare the child for any precise set of conditions" (Dewey, 1897, p. 77). As Dewey explained, attempting to identify some clearly knowable set of future conditions and prepare students for those conditions should not be the goal of education. This is particularly the case in the present age, given the dynamic, rapidly changing possibilities presented by digital technologies.

As such, it makes little sense to assume that we can accurately predict precisely what the future will hold based on what we know now. This, of course, presents educators with a seemingly unsolvable paradox: If we can only know what we know now, how can we possibly know how to prepare children for an unknowable future? One way out of this paradox is, as Dewey (1897) has explained, to cultivate children's capacity to take command of their own learning so as to better prepare them to navigate the ill-defined and changing nature of an unknowable future. One such capacity that can help children take charge of their own learning is creativity.

Indeed, creativity has long been viewed as a core cognitive capacity that can allow students to take charge of their learning, break from current habits, consider new possibilities, and, thereby, navigate uncertain futures (Craft, 2011; Dewey, 1934/2005; Green, 1995; Guilford, 1950). Lev Vygotsky, the famous Russian educational psychologist, underscored the importance of cultivating children's creativity by asserting that if a main objective of education is to prepare youngsters for the future, then the cultivation of the creative imagination should play a key role in the attainment of that goal (Vygostky, 1967/2004).

Mary Warnock, the British philosopher of education, presented a similar argument—asserting that the cultivation of students' creative imagination should be viewed as the "chief aim of education" (Warnock, 1978, p. 9). She went as far as to claim, "we have a duty to educate the imagination above all else" (p. 10). In more recent years, philosophers and scholars of creativity and education have made similar arguments. Sawyer (2010), for instance, has explained that students must be able to go beyond the simple memorization of facts and, instead, take responsibility for their own learning and work creatively with what they know to "generate new ideas, new theories, new products, and new knowledge" (p. 176). In short, life in the digital age requires people to be able to take charge of their own learning and contribute to the learning and knowledge of others—moving from consuming existing knowledge to creating and contributing new knowledge (Craft, 2011).

Clearly, there has been a steady stream of educational scholars who have highlighted the important role that creativity can (and should) play in preparing students to take responsibility for their own learning so as to better navigate and contribute to rapidly changing and unknown futures. So the question is not whether creative potential should be cultivated in the classroom (it should), but rather how creativity and academic learning are connected? I will address this question in the sections that follow.

THE LINK BETWEEN CREATIVITY AND LEARNING

Psychologists and educators have long recognized the connection between creativity and learning. As stated in the opening quote of this chapter, J. P. Guilford (1950), former president of the American Psychological Association, argued that in order to have a comprehensive understanding of learning one must also take into account creative insight and activity. Similarly, Jean Piaget, the influential Swiss developmental psychologist and learning theorist, asserted a strong link between learning and creative thinking—titling one of his books *To Understand is to Invent.*

Lev Vygotsky (1967/2004) also recognized this connection, describing a "double, mutual dependence" between the creative imagination and learning experiences. That is, creativity development requires knowledge and experience. Moreover, creatively thinking about one's experiences deepens one's understanding. As such, no creative act can occur without prior knowledge and experiences. We "never create in or with a vacuum" (Guilford, 1950, p. 448). Indeed, our prior knowledge and experiences influence how we interpret new experiences and serve as the basis for the development of new and personally meaningful insights, interpretations, and ideas (Beghetto & Kaufman, 2007).

Recognizing the link between creativity and learning can help teachers understand how creativity might play a more central role in their classrooms—complementing their teaching of academic subject matter and better preparing students to take charge of and contribute to their own understanding. In the sections that follow, several areas of convergence between creativity and learning will be highlighted, including: the constructive process involved in learning and creativity, the role of subject-matter constraints, and the importance of developing metacognitive knowledge.

Creativity and Learning as Constructive Process

A primary area of convergence in contemporary views of creativity and learning pertains to the recognition that both learning and creativity involve a constructive process. This connection is most apparent in cognitive-based views of learning. Although the specific processes, metaphors, and models of contemporary, cognitive-based views of learning differ (and sometimes quite starkly, see Tobias & Duffy, 2009), there is general agreement in the cognitive sciences that students develop their own personal understanding through a process of knowledge construction. Specifically, "new understandings are *constructed* on a foundation of existing understandings and experiences" (Donovan & Bransford, 2005, p. 4, *italics added*).

This process of knowledge construction is also central to the concept of mini-c creativity (Chapter 1). Recall that mini-c creativity refers to new and personally meaningful interpretations of experiences, actions, and events (Beghetto & Kaufman, 2007). Central to mini-c creativity is the "process of *constructing* personal knowledge and understanding within a particular social cultural context" (Kaufman & Beghetto, 2009, p. 3, *italics added*). This constructive process is illustrated in the following example.

Consider a child who is learning how to paint. She constructs her understanding of shading techniques as a result of a new and personally meaningful insight about how the combination of brush strokes and different hues of color create an illusion of shaded figures. In this example, the child is constructing a personal understanding of shading techniques on the basis of her mini-c creative insights. Recall that these insights may be new and meaningful only to the child. Moreover, the child's resulting understanding of shading techniques may be quite different from what is understood and done by more accomplished painters. Still, for this child, learning and creativity are working in tandem as she constructs an understanding of how to shade objects in her paintings.

Even at the higher levels of creative accomplishment (everyday to professional levels of creativity), recent theoretical and empirical work in the field of creativity studies parallels insights from cognitive and developmental learning scientists. Specifically, "process theories" of creativity (for an overview see Kozbelt, Beghetto, & Runco, 2010; Mumford, Blair, & Marcy, 2006; Ward, 2008) have, at their core, a logic that is tightly aligned with how learning scientists have described the process of understanding. That is, the new (be it an understanding or creative product) emerges from prior understandings and experiences. Whether in science, technology, art, music, literature, or other creative areas, creativity emerges from the conceptual combinations that have a basis in prior knowledge and experiences.

By taking a closer look at creativity and constructivist learning, teachers will be able to see how the two might be connected in their classrooms. Doing so will also help teachers recognize how this connection might be drawn upon to ensure that students are developing a deep and meaningful understanding of academic subject matter.

A Closer Look at Creativity and Constructivist Learning

The words "create" and "construct" are so close in meaning that they are listed in most thesauruses as synonyms. Not surprising, then, the link between creativity and learning is perhaps most clearly seen in learning theories that fall under the broad heading of *constructivism* (Plucker et al.,

2004). Indeed, contemporary constructivist views of learning recognize that "learning is always a creative process" (Sawyer, 2012, p. 395).

Constructivism, however, is such a pervasive and widely used concept that it is often difficult to keep track of what exactly people mean when they use this label. This is easily demonstrated by conducting a simple search on the Internet using the search term "constructivism"—resulting in more than three million hits. There is so much variability in how the term constructivism is used—meaning so many different things to so many different people—that is ends up losing its meaning.

In the present discussion, constructivist learning of academic-subject matter is not meant to connote unguided learning experiences (i.e., teachers stepping aside and letting students freely discover new understandings without any direction or guidance). Not only is there evidence that doing so does little to promote meaningful learning of academic subject matter (cf., Tobias & Duffy, 2009), most learning theorists who endorse a constructivist view would not characterize constructivism in this way. Indeed, attempting to get students to learn without guidance would likely lead to little more than "the acquisition of immature concepts and [the] neglect of important school skills" (Kozulin, 2003, p. 16).

The assertion that constructivism is synonymous with unguided, independent explorations is therefore more of a straw man argument advanced by critics of the view (see Tobias & Duffy, 2009) than an actual position held by many contemporary constructivists. Moreover, as most every teacher knows, this type of instructional arrangement would be considered a form of instructional neglect.

Interestingly, however, from a constructivist perspective, putting students in an unguided learning situation does not mean that they would not learn anything, but rather that they likely would construct an understanding of the experience very different from what the teacher intended. In a similar way, it would be equally inaccurate to assert that students do not construct an understanding based on more expository or direct teaching methods (e.g., a teacher standing at the chalkboard and guiding students through the recitation of answers to double column-addition problems). Rather, in such a case, students would still be constructing an understanding of this experience, but one constrained by the teacher's attempts to have students conform to what the teacher expects and wants to hear.

Thus, the concept of constructivism used herein refers to a process of learning that draws on the guidance and supports available in one's social-cultural-historical environment. In this view, students learn through a socially mediated process of subjective interpretation. As Cazden (2001) has explained, what students "internalize, or appropriate, from other people still requires significant mental work on the part of the learner. That mental work is what 'constructivism' refers to" (p. 77).

In this way, constructivism is an intrapersonal, subjective process that is reciprocally influenced and shaped by the interpersonal environment. As such, what students come to know is neither a mere copy of what has been previously known nor a completely unique interpretation of the student. Rather what we come to personally know might be considered "half-ours and half-someone else's" (Bakhtin, 1981, p. 345). Consequently, whenever students are engaged in a particular learning experience—regardless of whether it is narrowly constrained, wide-open, or somewhere in between— they will be engaged in a process of constructing some form of personal meaning of that experience. Even when students are required to parrot back responses to teachers, they will still have a surplus of personal under- standing of that experience that doesn't get articulated because students simply were not given an opportunity to express it.

If students are not given the opportunity to share, clarify, and refine the surplus of their personal understandings, they can come away with a prob- lematic message. Specifically, one's own interpretation is not what matters in school. Rather, what matters is whether you can arrive at the correct or expected response, even if you do not understand why. One's personally meaningful understanding takes a back seat to the appearance of under- standing, and learning is equated with the production of correct responses.

An example of how this might happen is when students are taught how to use a procedure or algorithm to produce consistently accurate respons- es, without adequately connecting it with their own personal understanding of when, why, and how to use such a procedure (Beghetto & Plucker, 2006). When this happens, students sometimes provide accurate, but nonsensical solutions to problems. Such as a student responding that "3 buses with a remainder of 3 are needed to take a class to the zoo" (Shepard, 2001, p. 1079). Although this answer might be technically correct, it has no practical meaning in the context of the actual problem.

Perhaps one of the best examples of why the ability to produce correct responses should not be viewed as a signifier of student understanding comes from the philosopher John Searle's critique of artificial intelligence. A key question in the field of artificial intelligence is how to determine whether a machine could be judged as being intelligent.

Alan Turing, the famed computer scientist, took up this question in a pa- per he wrote in 1950 (Cole, 2004). Turing asserted that if a machine could pass for a human in a conversation with a human judge, then the machine could be considered intelligent (or at the very least, it could be said that the machine exhibited intelligent behavior). On the basis of Turing's paper, the *Turing Test* became a common criterion for judging the intelligence of a machine.

The philosopher John Searle critiqued this claim by developing a thought experiment to illustrate how fooling a human judge should not be considered sufficient evidence that a machine is somehow displaying understanding or strong artificial intelligence. Searle's thought puzzle, called the Chinese Room Argument, proposes something along the lines of the following hypothetical situation.

Imagine an English speaking person who does not understand a word of Chinese. This person is placed in a special room that has a set of instructions, written in English, that enables the person to take questions posed in Chinese and produce accurate responses in Chinese. People outside the room send in their questions, in Chinese, and out comes the correct answer to those questions in Chinese. As Searle has explained, the set of instructions "enables the person in the room to pass the Turing Test for understanding Chinese but he [or she] does not understand a word of Chinese" (Searle cited in Cole, 2004, par. 4).

Searle's argument, used to critique claims about machines being able to demonstrate understanding, also serves the purpose of illustrating that the appearance of a student's correct response should not serve as a sufficient indicator of actual understanding (Beghetto & Plucker, 2006). Only by going beyond the veneer of correct responses can teachers recognize how students have constructed their understanding and, in turn, help develop and refine those understandings.

Going Beyond the Veneer of Correct Responses

An example of how eliciting the underlying understanding of students' seemingly correct responses can reveal surprising, idiosyncratic conceptions is illustrated in a videotaped case study of students' personal conceptions of scientific phenomena (Schneps & Sadler, 1987). In one segment of the video, a ninth grade science teacher is getting ready to watch a researcher interview one of her students (Heather). Heather is described by her teacher as one of the best students in the class.

Heather is seated at a table with a large sheet of paper and has a marking pen to help illustrate her answers. When prompted to share her understanding of the Earth's orbit (something she has been taught), Heather draws the sun and three planets (describing them as she draws). She identifies Earth and its moon. She then explains that the moon revolves around the Earth (drawing the orbital path of the moon around the earth) and that the Earth revolves around the sun (drawing an elliptical orbital path of the Earth around the sun). Heather then goes on to declare various additional facts using her diagram, explaining that "Each time the earth goes like this is a day [making a circular motion with her hand] and it takes … 365 days for the earth to go around the sun and that's a year."

At this point Heather has demonstrated that she is able to provide clear and accurate answers to the researcher's questions. Heather's teacher, who was watching the videotaped footage, states the following based on what she has observed to this point, "Yah, I would expected that she could give a better explanation than the other kids could...she's a lot more sure of herself...I hope she tells you what she knows."

If this were a quiz, and it had ended at this point, Heather likely would have received the highest score in the class. Indeed, based on Heather's response, a teacher may feel justified in making the inference that Heather understands the information and can, thereby, move on to another topic. Doing so, however, may fail to reveal the surplus of personal understanding that Heather has about this topic. By dwelling a bit longer with Heather, the researcher was able to go beyond the veneer of her "correct response" and allow Heather to reveal her own, personal understanding of this subject matter. This is evidenced in what Heather next explains.

After a few moments of looking at the diagram she had drawn (Figure 3.1), Heather pauses and then states, somewhat unexpectedly, "But the Earth doesn't quite go in a circle...it's more of...sorta like that (drawing a double figure eight trajectory of the Earth's orbit)..."it's more of...sorta like that..." Figure 3.1 is my attempt to recreate the surprising, double figure eight orbit drawn by Heather.

In addition to making the unexpected modification to her diagram (Figure 3.1), Heather goes on to share several misconceptions, some of which are quite common (e.g., Earth is further away from the sun in the winter, and closer in the summer) and other more idiosyncratic conceptions (e.g., Sunlight can bounce, and this somehow causes the seasons). Seeing and hearing all of this, Heather's teacher covers her mouth, shakes her head from side to side, and says, "I don't know, this is mind boggling..."

FIGURE 3.1.

Recalling the discussion of mini-c creativity, a student's construal of novel and personally meaningful understanding is, by definition, a creative process (at least at the subjective level of experience). In the case of Heather, her mini-c constructions—although novel and personally meaningful to her—were scientifically inaccurate and in need of additional refinement and alignment with the current scientific understanding of these topics. Heather's teacher, in collaboration with the researcher, was later able to help Heather clarify and better align several of her conceptions so as to be more scientifically compatible.

In the case of the strange orbital path, Heather was eventually able to identify how she combined (and confused) her understanding of the seasons, Earth's orbital path, and an image she came across in an Earth Science book for another class. The teacher commenting on the figure eight orbital path, while observing footage of a follow-up interview with Heather, was then able to recognize how Heather's conception of Earth's orbital path was not simply an in-the-moment confused response for Heather, but rather Heather's actual understanding. "I'm surprised she was able to remember the exact picture she had drawn. I mean she didn't even hesitate… And when we saw it originally it seemed to me like such a crazy thing. I mean that really was her idea of it" (Schneps & Sadler, 1987).

This example illustrates how important it is for teachers to go beyond correct responses and draw out students' underlying conceptions. Although students may seem to understand based on surface-level correct responses, they often have very unique, personal understandings of the subject matter. Moreover, this understanding may be quite different from their teachers' understanding. As such, it is important that teachers provide opportunities for students to share, elaborate on, and refine their mini-c conceptions so that they fit with academic subject matter conventions and constraints. By doing so, teachers can help deepen students' subject matter understanding (Donovan & Bransford, 2005) and develop students' creative competence by helping students learn how to move between their mini-c conceptions and little-c contributions (Beghetto, 2007b).

SUBJECT MATTER CONSTRAINTS

Another key area of convergence in the research on creativity and learning is the recognition that developing competence requires the development of subject-matter-specific knowledge (Donovan & Bransford, 2005; Kaufman & Baer, 2005). Contemporary creativity researchers and learning scientists are in general agreement that creativity and learning are subject-matter-specific. Indeed, spending time on content neutral exercises (e.g., come up with 100 new uses for a pencil) or some other form of mental gymnastics (e.g., practice memorizing nonsense syllables) likely will not strengthen students' creative or learning competence.

Learning for understanding requires experience working with and developing one's subject-matter-specific knowledge (Donovan & Bransford, 2005). As has been discussed in previous chapters, experts have more experience with subject matter knowledge and have developed deeper and better-organized knowledge structures of the subject area as compared to non-experts. This is why engineering experts, for example, are better able to reproduce a mass of circuits from memory as compared to novices who are unable to structure or organize the information (e.g., not recognizing the circuits as an amplifier) and, thereby, become too overwhelmed by the complexity of the task (Donovan & Bransford, 2005).

Similarly, with respect to creativity, subject matter knowledge provides the necessary constraints and content for creative thinking and the production of creative contributions. Recall, Guilford's (1950) assertion that no one is capable of creating in or with a vacuum. This is not to say that there are no domain general features involved in learning and creativity development. Indeed, contemporary creativity researchers have identified several factors that seem to influence creativity across domains (see Amabile, 1996; Baer & Kaufman, 2005; Plucker & Beghetto, 2004). Creativity researchers, therefore, have proposed hybrid models of creativity that attempt to highlight the combined role that subject-matter specific knowledge and more general factors play in creativity development.

The Hybrid Model (Plucker & Beghetto, 2004), for example, illustrates the importance of teachers recognizing a flexible or middle-ground position between domain generality and domain specificity. Teachers are advised to avoid extreme perspectives when it comes to simultaneously supporting learning and creativity. Specifically, this involves avoiding an over reliance on popular domain general creativity activities (e.g., "Try to come up with as many novel uses as you can for a piece of chalk...") or beliefs about creativity that are too fixed in particular subject areas (e.g., the arts). Instead, the focus should be on helping students develop their subject-matter-specific understanding and, at the same time, be encouraged to think creatively in and across various subject areas (e.g., art, math, science, and history).

Similarly, the Amusement Park Theoretical (APT) model (Baer & Kaufman, 2005) provides a framework for understanding how domain generality and specificity can work together. The APT model uses the metaphor of an amusement park to highlight how there are more general, initial requirements as well as different, specific aspects of the creative experience. General initial requirements include the right kind of environment, adequate motivation, and current ability level. These general requirements serve as the gateway into increasingly more specific thematic areas (e.g., language arts), domains within those areas (e.g., writing), and micro-domains (e.g., poetry) in which individuals can develop their creative and academic competence.

Hybrid models such as the two discussed above highlight the importance of developing subject-specific knowledge while at the same time recognizing the value of diverse experiences, flexible thinking, and the possibility of the cross-fertilization of ideas across subject areas. Complementing these theoretical models is research that has demonstrated how situating creativity in academic standards can simultaneously enhance creativity and learning. In a recent study (Webster, Campbell, & Jane, 2006), for example, researchers demonstrated the importance of striking the balance between unique student expression and sufficient background knowledge. These researchers examined the effects of teacher techniques on creativity during the invention of a new technology. They found that creativity was more likely to be enhanced in settings where there was enough flexibility and encouragement for students to be self-directed and when sufficient background about the topic was provided.

Similarly, John Baer (2003) has demonstrated in a study of middle school students that students enrolled in core knowledge schools (i.e., schools with a focus on academic content standards) had as high or higher ratings on creativity-relevant tasks (e.g., story writing, poems) as compared to matched students in non-core schools. Contrary to what some critics of content standards might predict, students in schools with more explicit content standards—and teaching that focuses on helping students attain those standards—are not necessarily less creative than similar students in schools with less-explicit content standards (Baer & Garrett, 2010).

This is good news for teachers who increasingly find themselves in standards based classroom settings. Indeed, teachers committed to nurturing student creativity need not view supporting creativity as an extracurricular effort (Aljughaiman, & Mowrer-Reynolds, 2005), but rather as part of their everyday curricular efforts. Rather than teach creativity as something separate from academic learning, it can be incorporated into everyday curricular assignments and assessments so students have an opportunity to develop and express their personally meaningful and unique understanding of academic subject matter (*cf.*, Beghetto & Kaufman, 2010b). How might this look in the context of an actual classroom?

Classroom Example

An example of how focusing on the development of deep subject matter knowledge can promote both understanding and creative ideation is illustrated in video segments from a 12-year study[2] led by Dr. Carolyn Maher and a team of researchers at Rutgers University. The Rutgers team was working with fourth and fifth grade students as they attempted to solve a set of mathematical problems called "pizza problems." These problems required students to identify all the possible combinations when given a set of initial constraints.

In one segment of the video (Harvard-Smithsonian Center for Astrophysics [HSCA], 2000), students were working in pairs addressing the question of: How many different pizza choices do customers have if they can select from four toppings? The students had the opportunity to develop and share their own unique and personally meaningful ideas (i.e., mini-c creative interpretations) for how to visually represent the problem in a mathematically accurate way (i.e., yielding little-c creative contributions).

The research team found that, after an hour of working on the problems, each of the nine pairs of students came up with at least one novel representation that differed from all other groups. Some students used stackable blocks to represent various combinations of toppings (e.g., yellow block on the bottom representing cheese, other colored blocks representing the other toppings). Other students made lists to keep track of the various combinations. Still others diagrammed their solutions on pizza-shaped drawings.

Working within the constraints of the problem allowed students to share and test-out their ideas until they were able to refine their mini-c ideas into contributions that others could recognize and agree on as being a viable little-c solution. This process, as I have discussed elsewhere, is called "ideational code-switching" (Beghetto, 2007b)—switching between intrapersonal mini-c ideas and ideas that others recognize as novel and meaningful (interpersonal contributions). Ideational code-switching is best facilitated by having clearly defined constraints such as those offered by the conventions of the various academic subject areas.

In the context of the pizza topping example, the combination of unique visual representations and mathematically accurate solutions provided the needed criteria for judging whether a contribution was creative (i.e., both novel and appropriate for addressing the task at hand). In this way, working with others and publicly vetting one's mini-c ideas helped to develop

---

[2] The 12-year research study commenced in 1984 and was carried out in the Kenilworth, New Jersey public schools in partnership with the Robert B. Davis Institute for Learning at Rutgers University. This partnership included a staff development program in K–8 mathematics. The videotaped footage is from the Harvard-Smithsonian Center for Astrophysics (HSCA) *Private Universe Project in Mathematics* and documents students participating in learning activities developed by the university researchers, after-school sessions, summer institutes, and individual and small-group task-based interviews (HSCA, 2000).

```
                    C.M.S

            C.B.P.S.              C.B.P.M.

            C.P.S.M.              C.S.M.B.

            C.B.M.                C.S.B.

            C.P.M.                C.P.B.

            C.B.                  C.P.S.

            C.S.                  C.M.

            C.P.                  C.P.

                      C.P.S.M.B.

                                        Key
            Cheese – C.        Peppers – P.
            Pepperoni – B.     Mushroom – M.
            Sausage – S.
```

FIGURE 3.2.

students' mini-c ideas into little-c contributions and also helped to deepen students' understanding of the academic subject area. This was evident in the culminating little-c visual representations that the students shared with their peers, teachers, and members of the Rutgers research team.

Figure 3.2 is similar to what two students (Marcel and Frederick) created as their representation for solving the problem (HSCA, 2000).

Figure 3.3 represents another example from a student named Brandon—who was in the "low ability math group" but came up with a particularly unique and insightful way to represent the problem (HSCA, 2000).

Brandon's elegant representation of the problem surprised the researchers and Brandon's teachers. This is because students, particularly students who are viewed as having lower abilities than their peers, often do not have the opportunity to "show us their thinking" (Maher in HSCA, 2000) and to develop and share their mini-c interpretations of what they are learning. However, when students are given that opportunity they often will surprise their teachers with the creativity and subject matter understanding they are able to demonstrate. As Carolyn Maher, lead research on the Rutgers' project, explained, "Children surprise us. They have wonderful ideas. They can represent their ideas in very interesting ways, in ways that would not even have occurred to us" (HSCA, 2000).

In the pizza problem example, students had the opportunity to develop their mathematical and creative competence. Competent performance is, as Donovan and Bransford (2005) have explained, "built on neither factual

P	S	M	Pepperoni
0	0	0	0
1	0	0	0
0	1	0	0
0	0	1	0
0	0	0	1
1	1	0	0
1	0	1	0
1	0	0	1
1	1	1	0
0	1	0	1
0	0	1	1
1	1	1	0
1	1	0	1
1	0	1	1
0	1	1	1
1	1	1	1

FIGURE 3.3.

nor conceptual understanding alone" (p. 6). Rather, competence develops when students have the opportunity to apply their knowledge in subject-matter-rich contexts. In the context of the pizza problems, students were challenged to go beyond simply learning and reproducing math facts and algorithms and, instead, were asked to: develop, apply, test-out, and refine their personal understanding of subject-matter-specific facts and concepts. Consequently, they not only developed and demonstrated their subject matter understanding; they also developed and demonstrated their creativity.

When teachers provide opportunities for students to share and refine their mini-c ideas, they will be in a better position to recognize how creativity inheres in the learning process, understand that each student has mini-c creative ideas, and gain insights into how they might better support the development of students' academic subject matter understanding. As Maher has summarized, "All children have ideas. And unless you know what those ideas are, you're not going to know what the appropriate intervention is, what the next step is, what the question is that you should be asking. Where to take that idea, to help the understanding grow for that child" (HSCA, 2000).

In addition to drawing out and working with students' ideas in the context of academic subject matter constraints, it is also important for teachers to help students develop their ability to take control of their learning and self-monitor their learning process. This speaks to how teachers can support students' creativity and learning by way of helping students to develop their metacognitive knowledge.

THE ROLE OF METACOGNITION IN LEARNING AND CREATIVITY

Recall Dewey's (1897) assertion that the best way to prepare youngsters for an unknown future is to help them develop their capacity to take command of themselves. This capacity to take command of one's self—in relation to learning—has been referred to as "metacognition" or the ability to self-monitor one's own thinking (Flavell, 1979; Pintrich, Wolters, & Baxter, 2000).

Metacognitive knowledge allows students to take control of their own learning, define learning goals, and monitor their own progress toward attaining those goals (Donovan & Bransford, 2005). The development of such knowledge not only helps students' future learning but also helps students develop their creative and learning competence in the present moment.

Metacognition and learning

With respect to learning, metacognitive knowledge helps support students' understanding and growing competence in a variety of ways (Donovan & Bransford, 2005; Flavell, 1979; Pintrich, Wolters, & Baxter, 2000). One way that successful learners use metacognitive knowledge is to monitor whether they are comprehending new information and, when they determine they are not, use strategies for increasing comprehension (e.g., "I'm not understanding this; I should probably re-read it." "I don't understand how this works; I need to ask one of my classmates or teacher for help").

Another way successful learners use metacognition is to explore whether and how new information fits with their prior knowledge and experiences (e.g., "How does this fit with what I already know?"). Yet another way that successful learners use metacognition is to test out one's understanding of academic subject matter with conceptions of their peers and teachers (e.g., "Here's how I solved the problem; what did other people do?").

An example of an instructional technique that focuses on developing students' metacognitive knowledge is *reciprocal teaching*. Annemarie Palincsar and Ann Brown developed reciprocal teaching to improve students' reading comprehension (see Brown & Palincsar, 1989; Palincsar & Brown, 1984, 1989). Reciprocal teaching combines the teaching of concrete comprehension strategies (i.e., coming up with questions, attempting to clarify new or confusing words, predicting what might happen next, and summarizing what has already been read) with opportunities for students to practice using these strategies on their own and with their peers. Teachers model these strategies to students, and students eventually take over and lead small reading groups using these strategies with their peers and are also encouraged to use these strategies in their own individual reading.

Reciprocal teaching can develop students' metacognitive knowledge because it provides students with opportunities to gradually develop their knowledge of reading comprehension strategies, which eventually become internalized and drawn upon by students to self-monitor their own reading comprehension when engaged in individual reading. The kinds of self-monitoring and strategies used in reciprocal teaching may be useful across a variety of subject areas. However, as Donovan and Bransford (2005) have explained, in order for metacognitive knowledge to be optimally effective in supporting student understanding, it needs to be taught and practiced in the context of specific subject areas.

There are various ways this can be accomplished. In science, for instance, students could be taught how to present and ask for scientific evidence when making claims. In social studies, students might be taught to think and ask about historical events from multiple perspectives (including the perspectives of different people, places, and time periods). In mathematics students could be taught how to demonstrate and ask for examples of the mathematical reasoning used for solving a particular type of math problem. Regardless of the subject area, the key takeaway from these various examples is that teachers can teach students how to take control of their own learning by providing subject-matter-specific strategies and practice using those strategies. Although these examples illustrate how metacognitive skills might help students develop their academic knowledge, it may not be clear why or how such skills could be used to develop students' creative competence.

Creative metacognition

Creative metacognition (CMC) has been defined as, "a combination of creative self-knowledge (knowing one's own creative strengths and limitations, both within a domain and as a general trait) and contextual knowledge (knowing when, where, how, and why to be creative)" (Kaufman & Beghetto, in press). This definition highlights the combined importance of self-knowledge, domain-specific knowledge, and contextual knowledge in relation to one's ability to self-monitor one's own creativity.

Creativity researchers have demonstrated both theoretical and empirical links between metacognition and creativity (cf., Kaufman & Beghetto, in press; Kozbelt, Beghetto, & Runco, 2010). Theorists highlight the link between metacognition and creative problem solving and assert that people who have higher levels of metacognition are more likely to generate creative solutions to problems (Davidson & Sternberg, 1998; Feldhusen & Goh, 1995). Although research in the area of CMC is fairly recent, there is evidence that accomplished creators have high levels of self-awareness about the quality of their own work (Kaufman & Beghetto, in press; Simonton, 2003). Beethoven, for example, demonstrated a high level of self-awareness in assessing his compositions (Kozbelt, 2007).

With respect to the classroom, there are several ways (adapted from Kaufman & Beghetto, in press) that teachers can help develop students' CMC and, in turn, support the development of students' creative competence. First, CMC is particularly important in helping students decide whether it is appropriate or worth the risk to share one's ideas with others. Teachers can help students develop their CMC by recognizing that although they may have a variety of mini-c insights when learning, it does not mean that other people will view these ideas as new, meaningful, or appropriate. In some cases this means that students may need to be patient and persistent—working with each other to help explore and clarify the value of each other's mini-c ideas. In other cases, this might mean that students will need to abandon a particular idea in favor of one that makes sense for the particular context. As Simonton (2003) has explained, the most successful creators are those who are willing to mercilessly weed their own ideational garden prior to sharing their ideas with others.

Teachers can also helps students recognize that creative expression involves some level of risk (Beghetto, 2007b). In some cases the risks will outweigh the benefits (e.g., writing a poem about the quadratic formula on an Algebra exam instead of demonstrating one's understanding of how to use the formula to solve a problem), and in other cases the benefits will outweigh the potential risks (e.g., sharing a new idea for how to efficiently solve a problem during a whole-class discussion). Teachers can play a key role in helping students increase their awareness of the positive and negative consequences of creativity. Doing so will help ensure that students can take control of their own creative expression and decide whether to take the risks necessary to engage in and share their creative ideas, insights, and interpretations. Of course, some students will need encouragement to take risks, whereas others will need guidance on how to take more sensible risks.

When students receive feedback from their teachers that helps them develop the knowledge necessary to consider the benefits and costs of creative expression, they will be in a better position to understand their own creative strengths and improve upon their weaknesses. This self-knowledge, as discussed earlier, is a core component of CMC. Teachers, therefore, play a key role in helping to develop this self-knowledge. Importantly, teachers will need to monitor and make sure that their feedback follows the Goldilocks Principle (Beghetto & Kaufman, 2007)—that is, ensuring that students receive feedback that is neither too harsh (stifling students' motivation) nor not firm enough (feedback that lacks information that will help students improve but is sometimes difficult for students to hear).

Finally, as discussed in Chapter 1, context plays a key role in recognizing whether people will accept (or dismiss) a student's original idea. Teachers can thereby support the development of students' CMC by helping students be aware of (and seek clarification on) the constraints for any given assignment, activity, or academic task (Beghetto, 2007b). Doing so will help ensure that students use those constraints as a guide for assessing the appropriateness of their original contributions (rather than be surprised or feel stifled by those constraints).

CONCLUDING THOUGHTS

The purpose of this chapter was to highlight links between creativity and learning. Three areas, in particular, were highlighted: the constructive process, the role of subject-matter knowledge, and the importance of meta-cognitive knowledge. These three areas are interrelated and stress the important role that teachers can play in making sure that students simultaneously develop their creative potential and meaningful understanding of academic subject matter. This involves providing students with opportunities to share their mini-c ideas and to receive informative feedback on whether those mini-c conceptions are compatible with academic subject matter conventions and constraints.

Providing students with opportunities to develop the kinds of deep and robust academic subject matter understanding necessary for the cultivation of their creative competence is not always easy. This is because teachers often inherit, as part of their own prior schooling experiences, highly convergent instructional practices that focus more on having students respond in predetermined ways than on encouraging the exploration and refinement of students' own conceptions. This situation is exacerbated by external curricular mandates that make it particularly difficult for teachers to feel like they can strike a balance between meeting external standards and allowing time for students to express and develop their mini-c ideas.

Consequently, creativity is sometimes in peril. Understanding the constraints that teachers face, however, is an important first step in considering alternatives for how to move from the convergent nature of schooling to instructional practices that more meaningfully include creativity as part of the everyday curriculum. This is the subject of the chapters in the next section of the book.

PART II

THE PERILS OF SCHOOLING

CHAPTER 4

THE CONVERGENT NATURE OF SCHOOLING

Now what I want is, Facts. Teach these boys and girls nothing but Facts. Facts alone are wanted in life. Plant nothing else, and rout out everything else.
—Schoolmaster Gradgrind in Dickens, 2008, p. 1

The Schoolmaster Gradgrind's view of education, as depicted in Dickens' novel, *Hard Times,* is the embodiment of concerns raised about how external accountability pressures have narrowed K–12 teaching and learning. Gradgrind's perspective stands in direct contrast to the idea that creativity can and should be cultivated in the classroom. Fortunately, most people do not share Gradgrind's view.

If you ask just about anyone the question: Do you think human creativity is important? You likely will find that the vast majority of people will almost immediately respond with a hardy, "Yes, of course!" The same is true for teachers. In my work with prospective and practicing teachers, I have never once encountered a teacher who felt that nurturing student creativity wasn't important. Why is it then that we often hear serious concerns about the suppression of student creativity in schools and classrooms?

One reason is that there is evidence that divergent thinking is suppressed in schools. The July, 2010 cover of Newsweek magazine, for example, had the ominous headline, "The Creativity Crisis" and included this byline, "For the first time, research shows that American creativity is declining." The Newsweek story (Bronson & Merryman, 2010) was based on an analysis conducted by Dr. Kyung Hee Kim, a professor at the College of William & Mary. Dr. Kim found in her analysis of more than 250,000 scores of American children on the Torrance Test of Creative Thinking that there was a steady decline in students scores starting in 1990 (Kim, 2011). The most significant decline was for students in kindergarten through third grade.

Of course, care should be taken when attempting to draw firm conclusions based on the results of one study, and even more care is needed when attempting to explain such findings. Still, the results do align with concerns put forth by some educational and creativity scholars about the systematic suppression of creativity in schools and classrooms.

CONCERNS ABOUT THE SYSTEMATIC SUPPRESSION OF CREATIVITY

At the heart of concerns about the suppression of creativity in the K–12 classroom is the assertion that accountability mandates have narrowed the curriculum to such an extent that teachers feel unable to support the expression and development of creativity in the curriculum. Professors Jeffrey and Lisa Smith (2010) have, for instance, explained that educational policies such as the *No Child Left Behind Act of 2001* "have sucked all of the air out of the ruminations of educators who might embrace creativity in the United States" (p. 252).

These concerns are not driven by a general dislike of assessment or accountability, but rather by how pressures from accountability mandates can serve to narrow the curriculum—resulting in a situation where teachers feel they no longer have the curricular opportunities or authority to teach in a way that allows for the exploration and broad development of students' creative and academic potential. Indeed, creativity seems to stand little chance in classrooms where teachers feel they have little to no instructional autonomy.

Professor David Berliner, for instance, has gone as far as to develop a new word to describe this phenomenon: *creaticide* (Berliner, 2011). Berliner defines this neologism as "The national design to kill literary, scientific, and mathematical creativity in the school-age population of the United States of America, particularly among impoverished youth" (p. 79). Berliner has explained that creaticide is the consequence of educational policies that have profoundly narrowed the curriculum, the assessments used to mea-

sure learning of that curriculum, and "a narrowing of the schools' conceptions of what it means to be smart in school" (p. 79).

Berliner's description of creaticide highlights the seriousness and depth
of the concern held by many scholars regarding the potential dangers and
pressures teachers face from contemporary educational mandates. The
idea of creaticide may seem quite extreme, particularly given that one's
creativity cannot really die. Indeed, as long as there is life, there is creativity. Still, the idea of creaticide serves as an admonishment to educational
policy and decision makers: If teachers continue to be pressured to focus
on increasingly narrow curricular goals, then creativity stands little chance
to flourish in schools and classrooms. Although such concerns pertain to
recent accountability mandates, the underlying concern that formal schooling can curtail creativity is not new.

Lingering Concerns: Creativity and Schooling

Long before the No Child Left Behind Act of 2001, research psychologists and educators expressed similar concerns about the stifling of creativity. John Dewey (1899/2007), for instance, explained that although we
often espouse a value for the creative imagination, we often undo much of
our talk because we hold too narrow a view about it—believing that the creative imagination is limited to "that of the unreal and make-believe, of the
myth and made-up story" (p. 72). The consequence of such a narrow belief
is a curriculum that ends up "not dealing with the living child at all"—even
though the imagination is "the medium in which the child lives... its every-
where and in everything" (p. 72). As such, connecting school to the child's
life requires that we give the child's creative imagination a meaningful role
in the curriculum.

J. P. Guilford (1950) also highlighted concerns about the potential for
creativity to be undermined in schools and classrooms. As Guilford explained, "We frequently hear the charge that under present-day mass-ed-
ucation methods, the development of the creative personality is seriously
discouraged. The child is under pressure to conform for the sake of econ-
omy and for the sake of satisfying prescribed standards" (p. 448). A few
years later, E. P. Torrance, the highly influential creativity researcher, raised
similar concerns. Summarizing findings from some of his earliest empirical
work, Torrance (1959) reported "we have seen many indications in our testing of first and second grade children that many with apparently impoverished imaginations seemed to have been subjected to concerted efforts to
eliminate fantasy from their thinking too early" (p. 313).

Torrance went on to document, in a series of longitudinal studies, what
he called a "fourth-grade slump" in the divergent thinking of approximate-
ly half of the children he studied (Torrance, 1968). Importantly, however,
many of those same students later rebounded from this slump, and sub-

sequent studies have found a variety of patterns in the development of divergent thought across grade and age levels (Claxton, Pannells, & Rhoads, 2005; see also Kaufman, Plucker, & Baer, 2008 for a discussion). What can be made of all of this? As I have noted elsewhere (Beghetto, 2010a), there are at least two important points for teachers (and other proponents of creativity in the classroom) to consider when interpreting the somewhat mixed findings on creativity development in schools and classrooms.

First, and perhaps most important for educators to keep in mind, the schooling experience does not necessarily suppress student creativity. Indeed, even for the students whose creativity slumped, Torrance later demonstrated that students could recover from creativity-stifling experiences (Torrance, 1970; Torrance & Gupta, 1964). This is important because it demonstrates that the suppression of student creativity in schools and classrooms is by no means a *fait accompli*. The schooling experience might, instead, be thought of as a crucible for creativity (Beghetto, 2009b). In some classrooms, students have the opportunity to forge their creative potential into creative contributions; in others, students' creative potential may be suppressed. The important takeaway point is: Although creativity can be suppressed, it cannot die. Even in the most stifling of situations, creative potential is present. It can be catalyzed and manifest—providing a powerful example of the transformative power of human creativity (Sternberg & Lubart, 1995). The potential for creative contribution is ever present, ready to spring forth and flourish. But it requires the right conditions (as will be discussed in Chapter 7).

Second, the issue is not whether the schooling experience impacts the development of students' creative potential, but rather how teachers might find a way to incorporate creativity into their everyday curriculum. Incorporating creativity into the everyday curriculum can be a challenging endeavor, given that there are a variety of potential roadblocks that can impede teachers' efforts. Teachers need to be aware of how these roadblocks might impede their efforts if they are to find ways to address them. In what follows, I discuss three common roadblocks (adapted from Beghetto, 2010a), including: the historical separation of creativity from the everyday curriculum, pressures from external accountability mandates, and inherited teaching practices.

Roadblock 1: Historical Separation of Creativity from Learning

One reason why creativity is often absent from the everyday curriculum has to do with the history of creativity enhancement in U.S. schools. Systematic efforts aimed at enhancing creativity can be traced to the early 1970s. During that time, Sidney Marland, a U.S. Commissioner of Education, was tasked with reporting on a congressional study aimed at exploring whether high ability students were appropriately educated in U.S. schools.

Marland's (1972) report represents a defining moment for creativity enhancement in public schools. His report noted that "creative and productive thinking" was one of six possible indicators of giftedness. Most importantly, the report provided a strong argument for a separate, specialized education of students who demonstrated high-levels of potential or achievement. The rationale for separating creativity from the general education curriculum was thereby instantiated in Marland's report and, in many cases, has been enacted in K–12 schooling ever since (Beghetto, 2010a). Consequently, sustained efforts to nurture student creativity have largely occurred in gifted and talented programs—separate from the mainstream academic curriculum. Aside from the occasional creative teaching and learning activities used by general education teachers, nurturing creativity has been a curricular responsibility of teachers in gifted education programs.

As I have discussed elsewhere (Beghetto, 2010a, 2013b), restricting the responsibility to develop students' creative potential to teachers in gifted education programs is problematic on several levels. First, when nurturing students' creative potential is viewed as separate from the mainstream academic curriculum, it can reinforce the stereotype that creativity is a trait limited to the elect few rather than a capacity of all students (Plucker, Beghetto, & Dow, 2004). Consequently, a very small proportion of students are typically afforded systematic opportunities to develop their creative potential. Moreover, this inequity is particularly pronounced for culturally diverse students who historically have been underrepresented in U.S. gifted education programs (Ford & Grantham, 2003; U.S. Department of Education [USDE], 1993).

Moreover, limiting creativity enhancement efforts to specialized curricula can reinforce a belief that nurturing creativity is not part of everyday academic subject matter learning. Even in gifted education programs that include curricula for developing creativity, there is often a belief that although creativity is important, it is somehow separate from academic learning (Beghetto & Kaufman, 2009). Callahan and Miller (2005), for instance, have described distinct, but interrelated, "academic" and "innovative" paths in their child-responsive model of giftedness.

Finally, focusing on creativity development only during some pre-specified time, with a pre-specified curricula, and in pre-specified spaces reinforces the problematic belief that creativity is something that can be turned on and off with the chime of a school bell. When teachers hold this belief, creativity enhancement efforts may be limited to a predetermined "creativity time" (Beghetto, 2013b) that otherwise competes with the instructional time reserved for academic learning. Moreover, when "creativity time" is separated from academic subject matter learning, teachers may be more likely to miss opportunities to develop creativity during the micromoments of the everyday classroom (cf., Chapter 2).

This, of course, is not to say that extracurricular creativity enhancement efforts are unimportant or have no value. Teachers can and do use predetermined times and spaces to help support the development and expression of student creativity. Moreover, there is research to suggest that structured creativity enhancement efforts can support the development of creative performance outcomes (see Beghetto, in press; Isaksen & Treffinger, 2004; Nickerson, 1999; Scott, Leritz, & Mumford, 2004). Rather, the point is that extracurricular efforts can and do play an important role when it comes to cultivating creativity, but they are simply not sufficient for developing students' creative potential.

Viewing creativity as extracurricular becomes a key roadblock to the meaningful and systematic development of students' creative potential. This is because, as was discussed in Chapter 3, the full development of students' creative potential requires that teachers recognize opportunities to support creativity in their everyday teaching and learning of academic subject matter. Unfortunately, the belief that creativity is somehow separate from academic learning is rather widespread. Indeed, it is a belief that even prospective teachers seem to hold.

Prospective Teachers' Beliefs About the Creative Imagination

A few years ago I conducted a study (Beghetto, 2008) exploring 176 prospective teachers' beliefs about the roles that the creative imagination and memorization of factual knowledge play in learning. As was discussed in Chapter 3, creativity and academic subject matter knowledge can be thought of as complementary. I, therefore, wanted to explore whether prospective teachers' conceptions endorsed this "both/and" view.

What I found was that more than two thirds (68.5%) of prospective teachers in this study indicated that there was a specific grade when teachers should place more emphasis on the memorization of correct answers (rather than encourage students' imaginative thinking). Moreover, a significantly disproportionate number of prospective teachers selected the elementary grades, and first grade in particular, as the time when students should be encouraged to focus more on memorizing facts as opposed to thinking imaginatively.

Of course, not all prospective teachers minimized the importance of encouraging students to think imaginatively while they were learning. In fact, nearly a third of prospective teachers indicated that it was never appropriate to emphasize memorization at the expense of students' imaginative thinking. Importantly, the results of this study also indicated that prospective teachers who viewed unexpected student responses as ideal were significantly more likely to believe that it was never appropriate to place an emphasis on memorization (at the expense of encouraging creative thinking). These findings are consistent with Greene's (1995) assertion that teachers need to embrace the unexpected if they hope to cultivate students' creative imagination.

Although there were prospective teachers who saw the importance of cultivating students' creative imagination in conjunction with helping students learn academic subject matter, a sizable majority felt there was a specific time in school that memorization should be emphasized, at the expense of the creative imagination. There likely are a variety of reasons why prospective teachers might believe this; however, I identified two beliefs that seemed to characterize prospective teachers' justification for their selections. Those two beliefs included what I called the "memorization-as-foundation" justification and the "memorization-as-time-to-get-serious" justification.

The memorization-as-foundation justification is a belief that memorizing facts early in school is necessary for creating a foundation from which students could later develop their creative imaginations. It was a justification often used by prospective teachers to explain why they felt it was appropriate to focus more on memorization in the early elementary grades. Examples of how prospective teachers used this justification for focusing on memorization in the early years included, "Start them out learning facts, and then with those building blocks they can use them for their own ideas;" "At an early age, children can learn how to memorize. As they grow older and learn more, that is when they can begin to really make opinions on what they are learning about;" and "Start memorization when they are young so they can have a good foundation so they can use the information to think imaginatively later on" (Beghetto, 2008, p. 138).

Although this justification has some basis in what proponents of creativity have asserted (i.e., the imagination doesn't occur in a vacuum, Guilford, 1950), it represents an unnecessarily limited view. Whereas this justification asserts a sequential, building-block view of creative development—memorize facts first, then focus on building creative ideation—it does not adequately represent the "both/and" recognition that the creative imagination and factual information can simultaneously support the learning of new information. Although creative thought draws on previous experience, it does not follow that this can be used as justification to emphasize memorization of facts devoid of the creative imagination. Doing so fails to recognize the important role that mini-c creativity plays in interpreting and understanding experience.

Consequently, emphasizing memorization without simultaneously encouraging imaginative thinking likely would strip the personal meaning and usefulness from that which is being memorized. Indeed, the imagination not only draws from prior knowledge and experiences, it also plays an instrumental role in understanding new information—particularly if what is being learned has not been directly experienced (Vygotsky, 1967/2004).

In this way, the creative imagination is used concurrently with memorization to meaningfully interpret the significance of experience and, in turn, make new learning experiences personally meaningful (Warnock, 1978).

As potentially problematic as the memorization-as-foundation belief can be, the memorization-as-time-to-get-serious justification is even more problematic. The time-to-get-serious justification is problematic because it implicates the imagination as being less serious, less mature, and potentially disruptive to learning. This justification is based on the belief that once children have had time to "play with their imagination" (be that in preschool, elementary, or the earlier grades in general), it is now time to get down to the serious business of learning (i.e., experiencing more structured knowledge and memorizing facts and correct answers).

Prospective teachers frequently used this justification for explaining why a focus on memorization was important at transitional grades (e.g., from Kindergarten to first grade, from early elementary to intermediate elementary, from elementary to middle school, from middle school to high school, and from high school to college or the workplace). Examples of how prospective teachers used this justification included: "Third grade [is the time to focus on memorization]... because it gives children enough time to play with their imagination, while catching them in time to begin teaching them facts;" "[Sixth grade] is when students are just getting out of elementary school, and it is time for them to start learning things by memorization;" "Eighth graders should be exposed to a more structured, factual style of learning that gets them ready for high school;" and "[By 12th grade] students will have been allowed to be creative and imaginative. So, now they need to be able to get correct answers for college placement tests" (Beghetto, 2008, p. 138).

The belief that the creative imagination is childlike, lacks any practical significance, and potentially distorts reality has long, historical roots. For instance, Plato famously denounced the creative imagination, crystallized in the form of poetry and the arts, in his Republic, because he felt it distorted the pure, essential forms of truth and beauty. Such views have persisted over time and, in some cases, have taken root in K–12 curricula. Recall John Dewey's (1899/2007) concern regarding a general tendency for parents and educators to view imagination as being limited to the make-believe. Vygotsky (1967/2004) similarly noted that the expression of the creative imagination is often dismissed in school because it is believed to lack any correspondence with reality and therefore lacks "practical significance" (p. 9). Moreover, Eisner (2002) observed that the creative imagination often fails to occupy a formal role in "serious" academic schooling.

In sum, the separation of creativity from academic learning has deep historical roots. This separation is so widespread that even prospective teachers seem to hold beliefs in alignment with this separation. As such, the tendency to view creativity and learning as separate serves as a key road-block when it comes to incorporating creativity into the curriculum. Understanding this historical separation can be helpful in understanding why creativity and learning are not easily recognized as connected and complementary. Moreover, this tendency to separate creativity from the academic curriculum may be more likely when teachers feel pressured by external curricular mandates. Understanding this historical roadblock in relation to the external pressures teachers face is a necessary first step in taking a more feasible approach aimed at integrating creativity into everyday teaching and learning.

Roadblock 2: External Pressures Placed on Teachers

It is true that creativity can and does thrive in the context of constraints—even the constraints provided by explicitly defined academic curricular standards (Baer & Garrett, 2010; Sternberg & Kaufman, 2010). It is also true, however, that external accountability mandates can place unnecessary pressure on teachers and students that, in turn, can serve as a key roadblock when it comes to expressing creativity in the classroom. These pressures become multiplicative when combined with the belief that creativity enhancement should be separated from the everyday curriculum. As was mentioned at the outset of this chapter, proponents of creativity have raised serious concerns about these pressures. It is therefore important to take a closer look at the basis of these concerns.

The most problematic feature of such concerns is the narrowing effect that such pressures can have on instructional practices and students' willingness to share their mini-c conceptions. Indeed, Guilford (1950) cautioned, "Let us remember…the kinds of examinations we give really set the objectives for the students, no matter what objectives we may have stated" (p. 448). Guilford's admonition is important to keep in mind because regardless of how teachers encourage their students to share their creativity, unless teachers also include expectations for creativity in their assignments and assessments, then students get the message that creativity really doesn't matter (Beghetto, 2010a).

When external mandates result in narrowed curriculum, then assessments used to measure learning are also narrowed (Berliner, 2011). These narrowed assessments typically take the form of fact-based tests. The increased use and importance placed on this type of testing makes it more likely that instructional practices will reflect the convergent nature of such tests. Educational researchers have noted this conforming effect. Darling-Hammond and Rustique-Forrester (2005) have, for instance, explained that the predominant use of fact-based tests "drives" instruction in ways that mirror the content, types of thinking, and representation of knowledge on those tests. Improving reading and mathematics is often the focus of external accountability mandates. Consequently, instructional time is diverted away from other subject areas and more robust and personally meaningful learning experiences.

On the surface, it may not seem problematic that teachers are spending increased time on mathematics and reading instruction. Indeed, if assessments are driving students to focus more on developing their content knowledge—something that is important both for learning and creativity—than what could be so bad about that? What becomes problematic, according to Berliner (2011), is how instructional time is often used. Specifically, there is often too much emphasis placed on superficial drilling or on superficial aspects of test preparation, rather than meaningful learning of academic subject matter.

Other researchers share Berliner's concerns and have documented how teachers often feel compelled to respond to external accountability mandates by narrowing their instructional practices. McNeil (2000), for instance, examined how schools have responded to externally imposed standardization mandates. She found that teachers' most immediate response was to narrow the scope and quality of course content—distancing students from more meaningful and active learning of that content. This curricular diminishment was most profoundly felt, according to McNeil (2000), by students who attended schools in low-income and predominately ethnic and racial minority neighborhoods—exacerbating longstanding inequalities in the opportunities and access to quality education afforded to traditionally underserved students.

The issue isn't so much with standardized tests, but how students' performance on such tests has become the focus of high stakes accountability mandates and how teachers experience the pressure of such mandates. Indeed, standardized testing becomes a barrier for creativity when teachers feel pressured by the belief that preparing students for such tests is their most important pedagogical goal. When the act of teaching and learning is reduced to presenting and reproducing factual bits of information, creative potential has little room to flourish. Many teachers recognize this problem and struggle with the pressure they feel to dramatically reduce the amount of time devoted to doing what they entered the teaching profession to do: encouraging, exploring, and developing students' unique and personally meaningful ideas.

The following description offered by a veteran teacher illustrates how teachers who face external assessment and accountability mandates feel (Groth cited in Berliner, 2011). Gary Groth, a classroom teacher with more than 30 years of experience, described how his most recent year of teaching was the "absolute worst year in the classroom" he ever experienced. Groth was quick to note that this was not the fault of his students, but rather the result of external mandates, "This year I was told what to teach, when to teach, how to teach, how long to teach, who to teach, who not to teach, and how often to test. My students were assessed with easily more than 120 tests of one shape or another within the first 6 months of the school year" (p. 85).

Of course, one teacher's experience is not representative of the experiences of all teachers. Still, even to the extent that the above description represents a worst-case scenario, Groth's experience illustrates the lack of agency that teachers can feel when faced with increased pressures to constrain and conform their curriculum to narrowly prescribed mandates—lacking the time, choice, or curricular freedom to engage in the kind of teaching that is conducive to creativity in the classroom.

Creativity in the Curriculum: A New Trend in Educational Policy?

If teachers experience accountability mandates as stifling their ability to support creativity in the classroom, then creativity may seem to have little chance to develop and thrive. But what if business leaders, educational policy makers, and government officials started to recognize the value of creativity? Might this recognition help lessen the pressures that teachers experience and broaden the scope of the curriculum? The answer to this question may be on the horizon.

In recent years, business leaders, government officials, and educational policy makers *have* started to recognize the importance of incorporating creativity into their nation's educational curricula (Craft, 2007; Ferrari, Cachia, & Punie, 2009; Organisation for Economic Co-operation and Development [OECD], 2008). One reason is that they recognize that cultivating creative potential of children is an investment in their country's future (Craft, 2007; Florida, 2004). Examples in the United States include initiatives such as the Partnership for 21st Century Skills and the federal government's "Educate to Innovate" campaign.

The Partnership for 21st Century Skills (P21) is a national organization that endeavors to cultivate "21st century readiness" in K–12 students by building partnerships among education, business, community, and government leaders (Partnership for 21st Century Schools [P21], 2011). The partnership has identified creativity as a core learning and innovation skill. Similarly, the U.S. federal government launched an "Educate to Innovate" campaign. The campaign is an effort among the federal government, businesses, non-profits, and professional societies to cultivate children's creative and innovative thinking as preparation for future work in the sciences, mathematics, technology, and engineering. In an address to U.S. business leaders, President Barack Obama asserted, "Our nation's success depends on strengthening America's role as the world's engine of discovery and innovation. And all the CEOs who are here today understand that their company's future depends on their ability to harness the creativity and dynamism and insight of a new generation" (quoted in Sabochik, 2010).

Not only have K–12 curricula identified creative thinking as a core student-learning outcome, but professional policy groups and associations related to higher education have as well. The Association of American Colleges and Universities (AACU), for instance, has asserted that "creativity…and the ability to apply learning to complex and unscripted problems are keys to America's promise" and thereby included creativity as a recommended student learning outcome in their report titled, *College Learning for the New Global Century* (AACU, 2008).

Although such "creativity in learning" initiatives may represent a welcome turn in U.S. educational policy, at this point it is too early to tell how policymakers intend to enact their desire to include creativity in the K–12 curriculum or the consequence of such policies. One thing that is clear, however, is that some sort of "No Child Left Uncreative Act" is one of the last things that America's teachers need (particularly coming off the heels of the No Child Left Behind Act of 2001). This is not to say that policies aimed at highlighting the importance of incorporating creativity in the classroom are necessarily problematic, but rather that external educational policy mandates often fail to take into consideration the realities of classroom teaching and, thereby, create a situation in which teachers are asked to add yet another thing to an already overwhelming and often contradictory set of curricular demands (Ingersoll, 2003).

In sum, meaningful efforts aimed at incorporating creativity into the everyday curriculum likely will not result from external mandates. Moreover, there is no evidence that policies aimed at adding creativity to the curriculum would replace external accountability mandates and pressures experienced by teachers. It is far more likely that creativity will be added to existing accountability mandates. This situation presents significant, but not insurmountable challenges for teachers. Teachers can still make important strides toward supporting the development of students' creative ideation while working within the constraints of academic content standards. Doing so, however, requires making slight but important changes to prototypical teaching practices (as will be discussed in Chapter 8). In order to make such changes, it is important to understand the nature and genesis of these inherited practices, as they can often serve as a roadblock to teachers interested in cultivating creativity in their classrooms.

Roadblock 3: Inherited Teaching Practices

Anyone who has attended U.S. public schools in the last century has likely experienced classroom teaching as being dominated by the teacher. That is, the teacher initiates the vast majority of the talking, poses the vast majority of the questions, and sometimes even provides the vast majority of answers. Hollywood movies have even satirized such instructional practices. An iconic example is from the 1986 John Hughes' movie *Ferris Bueller's Day Off*, in which a high school economics teacher (portrayed by actor Ben Stein) is featured standing in front of a group of disaffected high school students, intoning question after question, all the while providing the answers to his own questions. One of the reasons why this scene is so humorous is that it speaks to the experience of so many people. Unfortunately, the basis for this scene is not John Hughes' imagination, but rather a common instructional scene that has played out in countless U.S. classrooms.

Indeed, evidence from one of the largest observational studies of classroom teaching (described in Goodlad, 2004) empirically demonstrated the ubiquitous nature of classroom instruction dominated by teacher talk. The study included more than 1,000 elementary and secondary classrooms. Goodlad (2004) reported that, on average, 70% of instructional time was devoted to talk—with teachers out-talking students by a three to one ratio. Moreover, the vast majority of teacher talk involved telling students what to do; "barely 5% of this instructional time was designed to create students' anticipation of needing to respond. Not even 1% required some kind of open response involving reasoning or perhaps an opinion from students" (p. 229). These results highlight a legacy of instructional practices that are dominated by a teacher-centric approach to teaching and learning. Central to this approach is a focus on having students receive information from teachers with little or no opportunity for students to share and test-out their mini-c ideas and interpretations and develop those ideas and interpretations into little-c contributions.

Kenneth Sirotnick, a researcher who was also involved in the 1,000 classroom study, concluded that such instructional practices have long persisted in American schools: "We have seen that schools have changed little since we and those before us were there" (Sirotnick, 1983, p. 29). Moreover, there is evidence that such practices remain in place today and are not limited to the United States. The results from a recent multiyear survey of over two thousand 11 to 16 year olds in the United Kingdom (reported in Claxton, 2008) are illustrative of the continued legacy of convergent instructional practices. The survey asked students to select the three most common activities they experienced in the classroom. The most common activities reported by students were "copying from the board or book," followed by "listening to the teacher talking for a long time," and "taking notes while my teacher talks" (Claxton, 2008, p. 22).

What it is potentially problematic about these teacher-centric forms of instruction is not that teachers are directing the majority of the learning (this, in fact, is what teachers are typically hired to do) or even that teachers are doing the majority of the talking. Rather, the problem arises when students have little or no opportunity to share, test-out, and develop their mini-c conceptions of what is being taught. Moreover, as the former president of the American Educational Research Association, Lauren Resnick, has explained, these ubiquitous instructional practices—which have been used over the past century of schooling—"no longer suffice" because they are based on "assumptions about the nature of knowledge, the learning process, and differential aptitudes for learning that have been eclipsed by new discoveries" (Resnick cited in Claxton, 2008, p. 57).

In short, these prototypical-teaching practices are simply out of step with what is now known about how students learn, how students develop their creative competence, and what is needed to better prepare students for present day life, let alone a rapidly changing and uncertain future. Understanding where such practices originate and how they replicate from one teaching generation to the next will put teachers (and researchers) in a better position to recognize and disrupt such practices. The origins and reproduction of these practices are discussed in the sections that follow.

Origins of Prototypical Teaching Practices

Many features of the present day American school system were designed to prepare students for industrialized life in the early 20th century (Sawyer, 2010). This design was guided by a vision of schooling that had a goal of further populating industrial age factories. Educators during the time spoke directly about this factory influenced vision of schooling. In 1916, for example, education professor Ellwood Cubberley, who later became the Dean of Education at Stanford, described the role of schools using the following analogy: "Our schools are, in a sense, factories in which raw products (children) are to be shaped and fashioned into products to meet the various demands of life" (Cubberley, 1916, p. 338). Cubberley went on to explain that the specifications for designing instruction will "come from the demands of the twentieth-century," and it is "the business of the school to build its pupils according to the specifications... This demands good tools, specialized machinery, continuous measurement of production to see if it is according to specifications" (p. 338). This analogy has, in many ways, become the dominant vision of American public schooling and established the basis for a standardized approach to teaching.

This instructional approach aims to prepare students for the standardization of factory work. This is accomplished by requiring all students to "memorize and master the same core curriculum" (Sawyer, 2010, p. 175). This approach to teaching has been, according to Sawyer, somewhat effective in accomplishing its goals insomuch as it has eased the "transition from school student to factor worker" (p. 176). Where this approach clearly fails, however, is in developing students' creative potential and preparing the kinds of graduates "who can develop new knowledge and continually further their own understanding" (Sawyer, 2010, p. 176).

Although this standard approach to teaching is based on educational analogies and goals of a bygone era, many of its features are still evident in contemporary instructional practices. Consequently, the standard act of teaching and learning becomes one that can be reduced to a set of very basic instrumental practices: interpret, impart, and evaluate. Specifically, in this view of teaching, teachers are expected to interpret externally developed academic content standards—extracting the important academic subject matter that is codified in those standards. Then, on the basis of their interpretations of the content referenced in those standards, teachers are expected to impart their interpretations to students. Finally, teachers evaluate how well students are able to reproduce the content presented to them.

The act of learning, in this view, also involves three primary activities: interpret, align, and demonstrate. Specifically, students are expected to be able to interpret the lessons and learning activities designed by teachers, extracting the important academic subject matter that inheres in those lessons and activities. Next, students are expected to align their understanding with their teachers' understanding of the academic subject matter such that their conceptions fit with their teachers' conceptions. In order for this to happen, students are expected to demonstrate how their understanding matches their teachers' understanding.

Generally speaking, these basic acts of teaching and learning do not, necessarily, preclude the development of students' creative competence. Recall that creativity in the context of the classroom requires that students combine their original expressions within the context of academic subject matter constraints—and it is still possible to accomplish this, to some extent, in the confines of this vision of teaching and learning. The potential problem with this view of teaching and learning, however, is that its enactment can unnecessarily restrict the development of students' creative potential. This is because the goals that serve as the basis for this view of teaching have an overly narrow focus on helping students memorize and reproduce standardized content, rather than having the broader goals of simultaneously helping students deepen their understanding of that content and use that content to develop their creative potential. In short, if the primary goal is to match the teacher's conception of content, then conformity is reinforced and creativity is dissuaded. Moreover, rewarding convergent conceptions also has the unintended consequence of privileging students who have similar backgrounds to their teachers.

Consequently, when the acquisition and reproduction of standardized knowledge becomes the primary educational goal, it is easier to justify why class time is not used to go beyond memorization and recall of academic content. Indeed, this view of learning can place an expectation on teachers to not "waste" class time exploring how students are understanding the content or encouraging students to share their own, unique understanding of content but, rather, to use class time to cover as much content as possible and monitor whether students can reproduce that content in the way it was initially presented by the teacher. Such an approach to teaching is so widespread that it is likely to represent the primary instructional model of how teachers themselves were taught and thereby carry over from one generation of teachers to the next.

The Reproduction of Prototypical Teaching Practices

Before becoming a teacher, prospective teachers have developed robust beliefs, images, and assumptions about the nature of teaching and learning in the classroom. These beliefs, images, and assumptions start to take shape during prospective teachers' own prior schooling experience (Pajares, 1992; Richardson, 2003). By the time that the typical prospective teacher has graduated from high school, he or she has logged nearly 13,000 hours in K–12 school (Lortie, 1975).[1]

Recall that experts in a domain—expert chess players, for example—have, on average, spent 10,000 or more hours of deliberate practice developing their expertise (Ericsson, 1996). The amount of time prospective teachers have spent in school exceeds 10,000 hours and thereby can be thought of as a form of deliberate practice—shaping their images, beliefs, and assumptions about the nature of teaching and learning in classrooms. This is why the prior schooling experience of prospective teachers has sometimes been called an "apprenticeship-of-observation" (Lortie, 1975). This apprenticeship is quite different from the classic apprenticeship. Specifically, "the student's learning about teaching…is more a matter of imitation, which, being generalized across individuals, becomes tradition. It is a potentially powerful influence which transcends generations" (Lortie, 1975, p. 63).

Given that prospective teachers' beliefs, assumptions, and images are formed over many years, any problematic and potentially creativity-stifling beliefs can be difficult to shake. Consequently, such beliefs can carry over into current beliefs and, in turn, influence actual classroom practices (Borko & Putnam, 1996; Calderhead & Robson, 1991; Malmberg, 2006). In my own research and teaching, I have found evidence for a "carry-over effect" (Beghetto, 2007c) in a variety of prospective teachers' beliefs and practices.

In some cases, what prospective teachers have learned to imitate from observing their prior teachers will serve them well in promoting deep student understanding and developing students' creative competence. In other cases, the tacit knowledge learned in prospective teachers' prior schooling

---

[1] This average is calculated as 180 days of school x 6 hours of daily instruction x 12 years of schooling = 12,960 hours.

experiences will impede their best intentions to cultivate students' creative potential. The most likely situation is one in which prospective teachers have experienced a blend of positive and problematic practices. The challenge for teachers (and teacher educators) is to focus on those practices that are positive and address those that are problematic. Indeed, left unchecked, inherited practices can serve as a major roadblock for teachers interested in developing the creative potential of their students. Fortunately, once teachers are aware of these practices, they will be in a better position to make the kinds of slight changes necessary to simultaneously support students' academic and creative potential.

CONCLUDING THOUGHTS

The purpose of this chapter was to highlight how inherited beliefs and practices, especially in the context of increased accountability mandates, can present serious challenges to teachers' efforts aimed at incorporating creativity in their classrooms. What makes these issues particularly challenging is that we are not always aware of the beliefs and practices we have inherited from our own prior schooling experiences. Moreover, inherited beliefs and practices, coupled with increased pressures from accountability mandates, can create serious roadblocks when it comes to teaching for and with creativity in the classroom.

Taken together, the roadblocks discussed in this chapter set the stage for often inadvertent, but still problematic, practices that can suppress student and teacher creativity. Specifically, these roadblocks can fuel problematic beliefs about the creative expression of students and, in turn, result in creativity-stifling practices that undermine students' willingness to share and develop their mini-c creative potential into meaningful and contextually appropriate forms of creative expression.

Although these roadblocks make teaching for and with creativity challenging, the situation is not impossible. Teachers can still do much to support student creativity and learning in the context of these constraints. Ideas for doing so are presented in section three of this book (see also Beghetto & Kaufman, 2010b). Moreover, proponents of creativity, particularly at the leadership and policy levels, can also support teachers' efforts by actively questioning how such external mandates are experienced by teachers and examining how external pressures placed on teachers might be lessened. In the meantime, understanding how external pressures and inherited beliefs play out in the classroom is an important first step towards finding better ways to work with such constraints.

The focus of the next chapter is to take a closer look at a particular inherited belief, one that pertains to the nature of the educated mind, and how it can result in patterns of teacher-student talk that subtly suppress creative expression. Exploring the nature of this belief and how it plays out in the classroom will place teachers and other proponents of creativity in a better position to understand how and why students' potentially creative ideas are often dismissed and what kinds of things teachers can do to better support student learning and creativity.

CHAPTER 5

SOFT DISMISSALS AND OTHER INHERITED PATTERNS OF CLASSROOM TALK

No doubt [teachers] respect creativity, in the abstract, but not when faced with a classroom with 30 energetic children!

—Runco, 2007, p. 178

Mark Runco's tongue-in-cheek assertion speaks to the paradoxical situation that many teachers face: valuing creativity, but worrying that if creativity is invited into the classroom then curricular chaos will ensue. One reason this happens, as discussed in Chapter 4, is that our inherited beliefs can result in ambivalent feelings about the role that creativity might play in the classroom. Consequently, even though student creativity is generally valued, it can be inadvertently suppressed in the context of everyday classroom practices.

The purpose of this chapter is to explore how inherited beliefs about the nature of the educated mind can result in instructional practices that get in the way of supporting creativity in the classroom. Understanding how these

Killing Ideas Softly? The Promise and Perils of Creativity in the Classroom, pages 71–86.

beliefs can serve as the basis for instructional practices that inadvertently suppress student creativity can help to stave off the temptation to demonize or blame teachers for the suppression of student creativity and, instead, identify the taproot of such practices. This, in turn, helps put teachers, creativity researchers, teacher educators, and other proponents of creativity in a better position to address the basis for problematic practices, which can lead to the suppression of creative expression.

INHERITED BELIEFS ABOUT THE EDUCATED MIND

Many factors can influence how teachers teach. One key influence is the instructional practices modeled by one's former teachers. At the heart of these inherited teaching practices are longstanding assumptions about the nature of the educated mind. For the purpose of this discussion, it will be helpful to briefly revisit and elaborate on the inherited vision of teaching introduced in Chapter 4, what has been called the standard view of teaching.

Recall that the standard approach to teaching is one that involves transmitting factual information to students (Sawyer, 2010). The teacher's task is to deliver as much "ready-made knowledge" as possible to the individual student mind (Hatano, 1993) and then assess whether students can reproduce it (Beghetto & Kaufman, 2009; Sawyer, 2010). Driving this approach is what can be called an *acquisition-reproduction view of the educated mind*. Specifically, educated minds have accumulated a "great deal of the most important knowledge" (Egan & Gajdamaschko, 2003, p. 84) and can rapidly and accurately reproduce that knowledge (Beghetto & Kaufman, 2009).

One problem with this view is that it can distort how creativity is viewed in the context of the classroom and thereby preclude opportunities for creativity to be expressed and developed. J. P. Guilford (1950) illustrated this problem in the following, rather humorous, anecdote. A college instructor told his students that their term paper grades would be based on the amount of originality demonstrated. One student submitted a paper that was "essentially a stringing together of her transcribed [verbatim] lecture notes, in which the professor's pet ideas were given prominent place"— the student received an "A" with the added note, "This is one of the most original papers I have ever read" (Guilford, p. 448). As this anecdote illustrates, narrow assumptions about the educated mind may even distort what is considered original or creative. In addition to potentially distorting the meaning of creativity, the acquisition-reproduction view of the educated mind also restricts the expectations for how teachers should teach and, consequently, what and how students learn. Moreover, these inherited beliefs and the convergent teaching practices that emerge from such beliefs are so commonplace and so taken for granted that many of us are unaware that we have inherited them. Consequently, current and new generations of teachers may be unaware of the potential problems associated with such practices, let alone be aware of feasible alternatives to such practices.

Left unchecked, these inherited beliefs and practices can greatly interfere with teachers' best intentions to support student learning and creativity. Consider, for instance, the findings of a study of classroom teaching conducted by Dr. Kathy Schuh, a professor of educational psychology at the University of Iowa. As part of her study, Dr. Schuh conducted case study research in three middle school science classrooms. In one classroom, the teacher, Mrs. Chambers (a pseudonym), espoused a view of teaching that focused on promoting student understanding and collaboration. The teacher's espoused view, however, differed quite markedly with what her students experienced and what Dr. Schuh observed. The following description, reported by Schuh (2003), highlights the disconnect between what was espoused and what was enacted:

> Typically, science consisted of question-and-answer sessions... information was provided, and it was not always provided in a very compelling manner...I observed students with their heads on their desks as Mrs. Chambers talked—unusual in that some did not use their arms as a cushion between the desktop and their head—the side of the head flattened on the desk. (p. 430)

A teaching style capable of leaving students' heads flattened on their desks is clearly not in alignment with an approach to teaching that aims to cultivate student understanding and participation—let alone creativity (Beghetto & Plucker, 2006). Although this example is quite obvious, inherited beliefs about the educated mind can also lead to more subtle forms of convergent instructional behavior, as evident in the prototypical pattern of classroom talk that teachers inherit as part of their own prior schooling experiences.

THE PROTOTYPICAL PATTERN OF CLASSROOM TALK

The acquisition-reproduction view of the educated mind, which drives a more convergent pedagogical style, is clearly evident in what has become the standard or "default" (Cazden, 2001) pattern of everyday classroom talk. As I have described elsewhere (Beghetto, 2010a), this pattern of teacher-student talk is one in which teachers ask the questions, students respond, and teachers evaluate the correctness of those responses. This pattern of talk has been called the "IRE" pattern (Mehan, 1979) and is a micro-level enactment of the inherited model of teaching introduced in Chapter 4.

In this pattern of talk, the *I* of *IRE* stands for *Initiate* (this is the teacher's role, to initiate discussion by asking known answer questions), the *R* stands for *Respond* (this is the role of students, who respond one at a time and attempt to match what the teacher expects to hear), and the *E* stands for *Evaluate* (this, again, is the teacher's role and involves informing the class whether the responding student has provided an appropriate, correct, or acceptable response).

The IRE pattern is the instructional manifestation of the acquisition-reproduction view of the educated mind and, as such, is a rather efficient and common-sense strategy for delivering information to be acquired by students and for quickly assessing whether students have acquired and can accurately reproduce that information. Used judiciously, the IRE pattern of talk can be a quick and effective way to review and check students' ability to recall factual information (Cazden, 2001). The problem with IRE is that it is used so frequently during instruction and experienced so early by children (e.g., at home before children enter formal schooling) that it has become an iconic, habitual pattern of classroom talk (Cazden, 2001). The IRE pattern, like any habit, is difficult to break—even for people who are consciously aware of it and its potential to stifle creative ideation.

An example may help illustrate. When my daughter Olivia was 18 months old we were looking at a picture book together. My wife was videotaping the interaction with our new video camera. In one segment of footage from this home movie, I slipped into the IRE pattern of talk—assessing the correctness of my daughter's factual understanding of the images in the book (rather than exploring the basis of her interpretations). In the excerpt that follows, the letters representing the elements of the IRE pattern are added at the end of each utterance.

RB: "What's that?" (pointing to a picture of the moon)—I
Olivia: "moon"—R
RB: "Super job!"—E

[Several moments later]

RB: "What's that?...Look" (pointing to a picture of the sun)—I
Olivia: "Look at the moon."—R
RB: "That's the sun..." – E
Olivia: (turns the page, and looks away)—R
RB: (Turning back to the picture of the moon) "Let's look at that... there's the moon"—I
RB: (Turning back to the picture of the sun and pointing) "And what's that? What is that?"—I
Olivia: (Turns the page, disengages with the interaction, and starts playing with a pullout of an owl)—R

Somewhat incredibly, I was unaware that I had imposed the highly structured IRE pattern on this interaction with my daughter. My wife brought it to my attention, asking: Isn't that the type of talk you lecture your students about as being such a problem? Indeed. Rather than capitalize on a potential teaching and learning opportunity—by taking a few moments to explore and clarify how and why Olivia viewed the sun and moon as the same (e.g., both round, both in the sky)—I instead used my questioning to attempt to drive her to the correct response I was expecting to hear. The result: Olivia disengaged from the interaction. Given how clearly the IRE pattern is illustrated in this interaction, I frequently show this clip to prospective and practicing teachers when discussing lived examples of IRE.

Intellectual Hide-n-Seek

As has been mentioned, IRE becomes a problem when it is the default pattern of instructional talk. This is because classroom discussions turn into a game of "intellectual hide-n-seek" (Beghetto, 2007a), rather than an opportunity for students to express and develop their understanding of what they are learning. Consequently, teaching and learning are, in effect, reduced to a game-like situation in which students learn that in order to be successful—or win at the "game of school" (Fried, 2005)—they need to focus on puzzling out what the teacher wants to hear and how the teacher wants to hear it. This game of intellectual hide-n-seek is most evident in classroom discussions in which teachers' (often well-intended) efforts are focused on quickly covering content. Unexpected student ideas are therefore dismissed or redirected. The consequence of doing so can curtail creativity and inhibit student learning.

Paul Black and Dylan Wiliam, two education professors, reported on research that has examined the prototypical style of interaction that occurs between teachers and students during classroom discussions. Black and Wiliam (1998) have noted how classroom discussions serve as an important instructional opportunity for students to express and develop their understanding of academic subject matter. Unfortunately, such opportunities are often missed because of the common pattern of talk that tends to dominate during class discussions. Specifically, Black and Wiliam have explained that when teachers ask questions, they typically are looking for a predetermined response and use class discussions to try to direct students toward that expected response. Consequently, when teachers ask questions, they often do not wait long enough for students to think through those problems, but instead call on students who already know the answer or end up answering their own question (similar to the example of the teacher in the Ferris Bueller movie described in Chapter 4). This becomes a ritual that keeps the lesson moving at a rapid pace; simple fact-based questions predominate, students do not have the time or encouragement to think through and share their understanding of the subject matter, and meaningful engagement and learning suffer (Black & Wiliam, 1998).

Anyone who has participated in a class discussion likely will recognize this ritualistic and limiting pattern of talk. In a recent study (Beghetto, 2010b), I explored whether and when prospective teachers first experienced this pattern of talk in their prior K–12 schooling experiences. Results of this study indicate that the vast majority (all but one) of the 178 prospective teachers surveyed had experienced this pattern of talk and that the elementary school grades were most frequently identified as when prospective teachers first realized that successful participation in class discussions was more like a game of intellectual hide-n-seek (i.e., guess what the teacher wants to hear) rather than an opportunity to share and develop their own ideas.

Moreover, prospective teachers explained in open-ended responses that they learned several ideational inhibiting lessons from these convergent patterns of classroom talk, including (Beghetto, 2010b): It is not always safe to express one's ideas; respond only if you know what the teacher is looking for; never make eye contact with the teacher when you don't know the answer; and if you wait long enough, others will answer the question for you. Given that students seem to be introduced to this pattern of talk so early and so frequently in the schooling experience, those that go on to teach may have limited experiences with alternative ways to engage in teacher-student talk. Consequently, teachers may have learned (in their own prior schooling experiences) to use classroom talk as a vehicle for driving conceptual conformity rather than for developing students' creative capacity. This places their students' unexpected ideas in a tenuous position.

The Tenuous Fate of Students' Unexpected Ideas

The problem with unexpected ideas is that they can sometimes be viewed as too risky to warrant exploration. This issue was introduced in Chapter 2 and is worth revisiting here in order to understand how and why teachers sometimes choose to dismiss (rather than explore) unexpected ideas. Importantly, it is not just teachers who are uncomfortable with unexpected ideas. Indeed, the findings from a study by Blair and Mumford (2007) help illustrate this phenomenon.

In their study, Blair and Mumford asked participants to evaluate more or less original ideas. They found that participants tended to discount ideas that were risky and original and instead tended to prefer ideas that were "safe and consistent with societal norms and expectations" (p. 216). Blair and Mumford interpreted these findings by explaining that people tend to be risk avoidant, worry about potentially negative consequences that can result from selecting original ideas, view investment in such ideas as potentially irresponsible, and may even consider it irresponsible to pursue ideas that do not readily fit into pre-established norms.

In the context of the classroom, when a teacher is confronted with an unexpected idea, it is difficult to make the in-the-moment determination of whether the idea warrants exploration or redirection. Indeed, from the perspective of a classroom teacher who feels pressure to cover a great deal of academic content within a finite amount of time, exploring unexpected ideas may (quite understandably) be viewed as too much of a curricular risk. This is because encouraging and exploring unexpected student ideas runs the risk of taking the class off-track and into potentially unproductive directions. This may be one reason why teachers feel compelled to respond to unexpected ideas by quickly redirecting the discussion back to where the teacher initially expected to take it. This tendency to "stick with the plan" has been observed in research that has examined teachers' in-the-moment decision making (Clark & Yinger, 1977). Moreover, there is evidence that even prospective teachers tend to view unexpected ideas as potentially problematic.

In a study I conducted several years ago (Beghetto, 2007a), for instance, I found that prospective teachers seemed to lack comfort and confidence in dealing with unexpected ideas during classroom discussions. The 70 prospective teachers in that study generally preferred expected ideas (over unexpected or unique ideas), and the most frequent explanation offered by prospective teachers who held a low preference for unique or unexpected student ideas was that such ideas represented a potential—and in some cases, intentional—curricular distraction.

A prospective math teacher, for instance, explained, "Comments of this type may be intended to distract from the discussion" (Beghetto, 2007a, p. 5). A prospective science teacher made a similar, albeit more subtle statement in explaining, "I would probably like to stay on topic, but maybe it would be something we could pursue at a later time" (p. 5). In both instances, the prospective teachers viewed unexpected comments during classroom discussions as distractions that could take the class off-track. In the case of the prospective science teacher, the comment is softened by the qualification that perhaps the unexpected comment was something that could be pursued at a later time. Unfortunately, as anyone who has taught knows, there rarely, if ever, is a later time.

Of course not all prospective teachers in the study disliked unexpected comments. Still, they wanted to keep curricular tangents in check and harbored fears that such unexpected comments could easily take the lesson off-task. This combination of seeing value in unexpected comments, yet still having concerns about such comments, was illustrated in the explanation of a prospective language arts teacher: "As a new teacher, I fear getting manipulated to get 'off task' but I think when students feel comfortable enough to offer their thoughts, even if they seem way off target, this can give me a valuable insight to what they are getting out of the lesson" (Beghetto, 2007a, p. 7). Fearing that pursuing unexpected ideas will take the lesson "off-task" can, understandably, result in the redirection and dismissal of students' unexpected ideas.

Redirecting through Soft Dismissals

Given that unexpected ideas may come to be seen as potential disruptions, teachers sometimes choose to gently dismiss or redirect the class back to the planned lesson to avoid being taken off-track. When teachers develop this unconscious habit of looking for predetermined responses they, as Black and Wiliam (1998) note, not only inhibit student learning but also become less flexible and confident in their ability to deal with the unexpected. Consequently, when a student responds to a teacher's known-answer question in an unexpected way, the teacher may feel compelled to quickly redirect such ideas.

Indeed, one of the easiest ways to redirect students' unexpected ideas is to gently dismiss those ideas. Kennedy (2005), for instance, reported from her study of elementary teachers that one of the most common strategies used in response to students' "off-script" comments was to gently dismiss such comments by saying, "We'll talk about this later" (p. 120). Such "soft dismissals" (Beghetto, 2009b) may even involve noting that a student's idea is creative (e.g., "That's a creative way to think about it...") and in the same breath bring the discussion back on the expected curricular path (e.g., "... Now, let's get back on track."). Again, this is not to say that such soft dismissals are never warranted or appropriate. Rather, soft dismissals become problematic when they occur with regularity (Beghetto, 2009b). This is because such dismissals can, over time, send a message to students that their mini-c ideas are not welcome and thereby curtail students' willingness to share their mini-c ideas, interpretations, and understandings.

Results of a study that examined students' creative self-beliefs (Beghetto, 2006), for example, indicate that although more creatively inclined students reported that their teachers told them they were creative, they were also significantly more likely to report that their teachers didn't really listen to them and had given up on them. It would seem that, in some instances, teachers telling students they are "creative" may sometimes be a way to gently or indirectly let students know that their ideas are off-base, not worth listening to, and not aligned with what their teacher expects or wants to hear.

Again, it is important to note that teachers' dismissals of students' unexpected ideas likely are not driven by an overt dislike of creativity or creative students. Rather, it is more likely that teachers dismiss unexpected ideas somewhat habitually because such ideas represent curricular uncertainty and potential curricular distractions. However, such an instructional move—while understandable—is still problematic. As Kennedy (2005) has explained, "The problem with dismissals is self-evident...they give students a clear message that some ideas won't be talked about, even if they seem relevant and important to students. Dismissals clearly discourage students from investing intellectual energy in their learning" (p. 120). Moreover, as will be discussed in the examples that follow, soft dismissals come at the cost of sealing off micromoment opportunities to explore and develop students' understanding and creative potential.

Classroom Examples

The following excerpts from actual classrooms may help illustrate how students' ideas are dismissed (sometimes subtly, other times more obviously) when teachers use question-and-answering to drive students toward a conception that conforms with the teachers' preexisting conceptions. This first example illustrates a rather obvious use of question-and-answering to drive students to conform to what the teacher wants to hear. The excerpt is from a dialogue a teacher had with a small group of elementary school students during a reading lesson (adapted from Skidmore cited in Matusov, 2009, pp. 113–114):

Teacher: Right. So is it true or false? Rocky knew the sound ..erm... "He heard a dog barking." Did he hear in the first picture on the first page did he hear that barking to be a dog?

Fiona: Yes.

Teacher: It wasn't a dog... Fiona. It was false because it was a fox barking. How does he know it was a fox barking? 'Cause he described it to Mr. Keeping later on and Mr. Keeping said ha that's a fox bark. Fox... foxes bark like that. Do you understand? No really do you?

Fiona: Erm. (Fiona *shakes her head*).

Teacher: Why do you think that it's a dog barking? You tell me one piece of information from that story to tell you that it's a dog.

Fiona: Because... erm... foxes don't bark and dogs does... do.

Teacher: OK, look at page six Fiona. Page six? OK. Read it with me.

Teacher and Fiona: "The next day Rocky saw Mr. Keeping. He told him about the noise."

Teacher: What noise, Fiona? What noise?

Fiona: The noise what the fox was making.

Teacher: The noise that the fox was making. Which noise was the fox making?

Fiona: A dog... noise. (Fiona *laughs*).

Teacher: He was barking. The fox was barking, yeah? So the noise that he heard in the night. So he told him about the noise. Carry on... reading... page six. "That"

Teacher and Fiona: "will be a fox said Mr. Keeping. Foxes bark like that."

Teacher: So. So the noise he heard on that first page was a bark. He thought it might have been a dog.
Fiona: It wasn't.
Teacher: But it wasn't a dog. What was it?
Fiona: He knew it wasn't a dog.
Teacher: What was it?
Fiona: It was a fox.
Teacher: It was a fox. And the statement says on your sheet "He heard a dog barking." Did he hear a dog barking? So is it true or false?
Fiona: False.
Teacher: Do you understand?
Fiona: Yes.
Teacher: OK, next sentence.

The teacher in the above segment seems to be using questions and answers to drive the student toward what the teacher already has in mind. The problem here is not that the teacher wants to help Fiona understand the answer to the true/false question, but rather that the singular focus on driving toward that outcome precludes opportunities for acknowledging and exploring Fiona's conceptions. Consequently, Fiona comes to learn that the goal of the question-and-answering is not really about what she thinks, but rather about reproducing what the teacher wants to hear. In lines six and twelve of the above dialogue, for example, Fiona attempts to convey why she responded to the true/false question as she did (based on her prior understanding and experiences with dogs and foxes). Fiona laughs at line twelve, perhaps indicating that she is resisting this reproduction of what the teacher wants. Fiona eventually acquiesces and, by line sixteen, demonstrates the compliant cognition that the teacher is after. The teacher then goes on for an additional nine lines of dialogue to seemingly cement Fiona's compliance.

The teacher uses a special form of questioning used to drive the student to the teacher's predetermined conception. Eugene Matusov, a professor of education, has described these types of questions as "known-answer questions," and they are used to guide students to "know what the teacher already knows" and aimed at "students' affirmation of the teacher's knowledge" rather than an exploration and development of the students' own insights and interpretations (Matusov, 2009, p. 113). In any other context, the use of such questions would be viewed as incredibly bizarre, insulting, and even manipulative. This can be illustrated in a simple thought experiment.

Imagine you are with a group of friends and discussing ideas for where you might go out to eat dinner. What would happen if you tried using known-answer questions to guide the group toward affirming your predetermined choice? Imagine asking them where they would like to eat and when they were not able to successfully guess what you wanted to hear you say something like, "Nope. Try again" or "No, that's not correct. How about you try to think about what I like to eat and then tell me where you want to go?" Imagine how your friends would respond to such a thinly veiled attempt at coercing them to your predetermined selection. You likely would need to abandon this strategy (unless you wanted to damage your relationship with them).

Even though this questioning strategy is socially awkward outside of the classroom, it is quite commonplace in the classroom, used unconsciously by teachers and replicated from one generation of teachers to the next. This pattern of talk is so iconic that kids playing school often reproduce it. It simply is the way teachers talk. Once teachers become aware of this pattern of talk, the creativity-stifling effects are obvious, and teachers can work toward consciously disrupting this pattern.

Questions to drive students toward preconceived conceptions and expectations are, however, not always this obvious. Sometimes a more subtle approach is taken in which students are asked to share their ideas in a more open ended or even seemingly brainstorming format (i.e., "all ideas are welcome"). As the next example illustrates, however, even a more open ended, brainstorming style of questioning can still be used to move students to expected responses. The following excerpt is from video footage of a sixth grade science lesson (Hannah & Abate, 1995). The excerpt is from the beginning of the lesson, in which the teacher is reviewing content prior to engaging students in a hypothesis testing activity:

Teacher: I need someone to tell me what a hypothesis is.
Student: A what…a what?
Teacher: [stressing each syllable] A Hy-Poth-E-sis. What do you THINK that word is? We have talked about it a little bit before. Andrea, what do you think it means?
Andrea: [softly] A plant.
Teacher: A plan. That's a good guess…
Andrea: [louder] Plan-T.
Teacher: A plant!? [look of surprise] Ok, we'll put that up. [writing "plant" on the chalkboard]. I'm going to put every answer up and we'll try to see…what we've got. What else, Tim?
Tim: A hard word to say.
Teacher: Ok [chuckling, rolling eyes] it's a hard word.
Teacher: Felton, what do you think it is?
Felton: [inaudible]
Teacher: Ok, maybe a kind of animal…we're kinda getting off the track. We have had this word before…Ok, Stephanie?

Stephanie: A type of dictionary or something?

[After several more incorrect guesses from students]

Teacher: Rob what do you think?
Rob: I think it's a kind of idea.
Teacher: Ok, kind of an idea...I'm gonna stop right there 'cause Rob did come up with it.

As illustrated in the above example, even when teachers genuinely encourage all students to share their ideas, it is still possible for the discourse to slip into a game of intellectual hide-n-seek. Even though the teacher in the above excerpt invites students to share what they think, her subsequent pattern of questioning and responding to students suggests, instead, that she is really more interested in students providing a response that conforms closely enough with *her* conception of hypothesis.

Specifically, by responding to student responses by looking surprised and by redirecting ("we're kinda getting off-track," "we've had this word before," and "I'm gonna stop...'cause Rob did come up with it"), the teacher signals to her students that the actual goal of this question-and-answer session is not what she initially stated (i.e., wanting to hear what students *think* the word hypothesis means) but, rather, whether they can come up with what she wants to hear.

One reason why the enactment of seemingly open ended, brainstorming-like interactions can devolve into a game of intellectual hide-n-seek is that teachers are (somewhat understandably) focused on covering requisite content so they can move on to some other learning objective or activity, rather than focus on what is happening in the actual moment. In the case of the above example, for instance, it could be that the teacher wanted to get students to start the hypothesis testing activity so they didn't run out of time.

In this way, lesson plans can have the unintended consequence of focusing teachers attention on what is next in the sequence, rather than what is happening in the moment. The above segment not only illustrates how seemingly open ended question-and-answer sessions can move students to what teachers want to hear, but also serves as a subtle form of ideational dismissal. The approach used by this teacher is less direct then the one used by the reading teacher in the earlier example; still this less direct approach has the same outcome: moving students to what the teacher wants to hear.

When teachers are focused on moving students to predetermined conceptions, they may hear what they expect to hear rather than what students are actually saying. In the above excerpt, for instance, Andrea says "plant," but the teacher hears "plan." The student, however, clarifies that what she initially said was "plant"—stressing the "t." The teacher seems surprised by this, perhaps because *plan* is something that she could have worked with to help move students toward her conception of hypothesis. It is not until several turns later that the teacher hears from Rob a response she can work with: "a kind of idea."

In addition to moving students toward existing conceptions, this pattern of talk can result in students' ideas being discounted or dismissed. Returning to the exchange in line five of the above dialogue, when Andrea clarifies that what she actually said was *plant*, the teacher was confronted with a micromoment decision: Do I spend class time exploring this particular response or softly dismiss it and move on? Although the teacher writes the student's response on the chalkboard, she is actually doing so as a way of gently dismissing Andrea's response. This is because she never seeks to understand the basis of this response. As such, the chalkboard becomes an ideational graveyard—where ideas that do not fit expectations are placed and eventually buried-under by chalk dust.

Although it is likely that Andrea may have been signifying her confusion when she offered "plant," it is also possible that she had some relevant association between plant and hypothesis. Unfortunately, because the teacher did not take a moment to explore this idea, it is impossible to determine whether this idea emerged out of the student's confusion or a relevant association with a prior learning experience. Recall from Chapter 3 that mini-c insights sometimes take a few minutes of teacher-guided exploration for students to be able to fully articulate their ideas in a way that helps the teacher (and sometimes even students themselves) recognize whether their ideas fit the discussion at hand. When teachers invite students to share their ideas (e.g., "I'm gonna put everyone's ideas up here to see what we've got") but fail to take time to briefly explore those ideas, they can, inadvertently, send the message to students that what they are *really* looking for when they invite ideas is not what students think, but rather whether students can guess what the teacher expects to hear.

ALTERNATIVES TO TEACHING FOR CONCEPTUAL CONFORMITY

As has been discussed, teachers sometimes are socialized by their own prior schooling experiences to use question-and-answer routines in creativity curtailing ways. Rather than promote expression and exploration of ideas, these routines reinforce the importance of conforming to teachers' expectations and preexisting conceptions. When this happens, student creativity and meaningful learning suffer.

Alternatively, teachers who teach for creativity recognize that such a conformity driven approach is problematic. They also recognize that teaching for creativity does not mean abandoning academic subject matter constraints or learning outcomes. Instead, they focus on orchestrating subject-matter-rich opportunities for students to develop personal understandings that are compatible with existing knowledge—leaving room for the encouragement and exploration of students' mini-c understanding of the academic subject matter being taught.

Teaching from this perspective still involves teachers relating their conception of subject matter to students and encouraging students to share and develop compatible conceptions, but doing so without forcing a shared conception. In this way teachers can help students develop a personally meaningful understanding that is compatible with existing knowledge and keep the door open for the possibility of expanding on existing knowledge. This requires that teachers encourage a more exploratory approach when engaging students in problem solving tasks.

As discussed in Chapters 2 and 4, when teachers take the time to explore unexpected student ideas and other surprising turns in the curriculum, creativity flourishes. Recall the student (Sean) who was willing to share and able to persist in developing the highly unexpected, yet viable, concept of how some numbers can be both odd and even. Or recall the students who were willing to share multiple unique and mathematically accurate solutions when given the time and support to articulate and develop their mini-c conceptions. The common theme across these examples is that their teachers took a few moments to encourage and explore the unexpected ideas presented by these students.

Researchers have also demonstrated how creative ideation is more likely to be expressed when an exploratory (rather than a more direct or convergent) approach is adopted (Beghetto, Kaufman, Hegarty, Hammond, & Wilcox-Herzog, 2012). Consider, for example, the results of a recent study conducted with a group of young children (Buchsbaum, Gopnick, Griffiths, & Shafto, 2010). The researchers set up an experiment in which they provided two groups of young children (four-year-olds) with a toy that plays music. In the first group the researcher portrayed a more exploratory approach ("This is my new toy ... but I haven't played with it yet, so I don't know how to make it go"; "What if I ..."; "Why don't you try ...") to demonstrating the toy. In the second group, the researchers portrayed a more direct approach ("See this toy? This is my toy, and it plays music. I'm going to show you how it works."). The students in the first group were more likely to generate novel ways of getting the toy to work, whereas students in the second group were more likely to simply imitate the modeled steps demonstrated by the researcher.

In a related study (Bonawitzj et al., 2010), researchers presented two groups of four-year-old children with a toy that had features that could be active (e.g., sounds and lights). With one group of children the researchers took a more direct approach ("Look at my toy! This is my toy! I'm going to show you how my toy works. Watch this!"). With the second group of children they took a more exploratory approach ("I just found this toy! See this toy?" "Huh! Did you see that?" acting surprised when activating one of its features). The researchers then invited both groups of children to play with the toy. The children who experienced a more exploratory approach were more likely than their peers who experienced a more direct approach to engage in exploratory, curiosity driven behaviors that resulted in more novel discoveries.

Taken together, these examples illustrate the potential benefits of taking a more exploratory approach to teaching. Adopting such an approach is one way that teachers can disrupt inherited patterns of classroom talk that tend to stifle creative expression. Indeed, approaching students' unexpected ideas with curiosity and willingness to briefly explore those ideas can go a long way in communicating to students that it is worth the risk to share and develop their own mini-c conceptions.

CONCLUDING THOUGHTS

The purpose of this chapter was to highlight how inherited beliefs about the educated mind can result in the use of creativity-stifling patterns of teacher-student talk. Specifically, the acquisition-reproduction view of the educated mind can lead to patterns of instructional talk that make it difficult for teachers and students to explore and develop unexpected ideas into meaningful classroom contributions.

Given that teachers have a lot of curricular ground to cover and limited time to cover it, they may understandably be more focused on driving students in the direction of the next item on the lesson plan. Moreover, as discussed in Chapter 4, this focus on covering content is further exacerbated by external accountability mandates that place increased pressure on teachers to get all students to predetermined outcomes in preparation for standardized assessments. When this happens, teachers' questions are not invitations for students to share their ideas, insights, or interpretations, but, rather, a means for helping guide students to what the teacher wants to hear. In such situations, unexpected student ideas represent more of a distraction than a learning opportunity.

Left unchecked these inherited patterns of classroom talk can result in students learning that it is more important to focus on attempting to conform to the preexisting and expected conceptions of their teachers, rather than take the risk to share and develop their own understanding and creative capacity. Fortunately, teachers can disrupt this creativity-stifling pattern of talk by adopting a more exploratory approach to students' unexpected ideas.

Additional examples of the kinds of strategies and approaches conducive to creativity and meaningful learning are presented in Part Three of the book. Before exploring such practices and strategies, however, it is important to explore the role that evaluative feedback plays in determining whether students' creativity will be supported or suppressed. This is the focus of the next chapter.

CHAPTER 6

CREATIVE MORTIFICATION

*But should the day ever come when thee sees thy most cherished ambition dashed
to the ground like a potter's vessel, then will thee understand me.*
                                              —Davis & Stratton, 2010, p. 106

Teachers make countless evaluative decisions each day. Sometimes these
decisions result in providing positive feedback. Other times they involve
pointing out students' mistakes. Sometimes this feedback involves lengthy
explanations. Other times it involves nothing more than a look or saying
and doing nothing at all. A key question that teachers might have about
their feedback is how it might influence student creativity. More specifically, is it possible for a student's creative ambition to be dashed, shattered
to the ground like a potter's vessel as described in the opening quote? Is
the above description simply an example of artistic hyperbole, or is this
something that should concern educators? Might it be possible for a seemingly throwaway evaluative comment—from a teacher, parent, or coach—to
result in such a profoundly stifling experience for students?

   One way to approach this question is to first recognize that there is no
compelling evidence to suggest that one's creativity can be permanently
eliminated. Recall that even in cases where there seemed to have been

the systematic suppression of student creativity (Torrance, 1968), many of those same students were later found to be able to bounce back (Torrance, 1970; Torrance & Gupta, 1964). Importantly, however, it is still possible for a child's creativity to be profoundly stifled. There are circumstances whereby a single, momentary evaluation of a student's creative expression can have long-lasting and profoundly detrimental effects on his or her subsequent creative expression—suspending the further development of that student's creative potential. This has been called *creative mortification* (Beghetto, 2011).

Creative mortification refers to the indefinite suspension of someone's creative expression. A student who aspires to be a poet, for instance, may stop writing poetry after having received harsh evaluative feedback from a trusted teacher. Of course not all students who receive negative, even harsh, evaluative feedback will stop writing; some may in fact be inspired and write even more after such feedback. How might this be the case? This chapter will explore this question.

UNDERSTANDING CREATIVE MORTIFICATION

Creative mortification (CM) is a form of profound creative suppression resulting from a shaming experience (Beghetto, 2011). Creative mortification often occurs after having experienced negative evaluative feedback. Such feedback can occur in a brief, fleeting moment. Central to the experience of creative mortification is a crushing of the creative spirit. Creativity itself does not die. What dies is one's creative will. As a result, someone who experiences creative mortification is no longer willing to share, develop, or identify with what used to be an enjoyable and personally meaningful form of creative expression. What was once a creative aspiration becomes little more than a painful memory.

Over the years, I started gathering first-hand accounts of creative mortification. I started with more informal settings, such as discussions with friends or guests at a dinner party. I then started gathering accounts in more formal settings and venues, such as audience members attending an invited lecture or as a topic of discussion in the college courses I teach. I have also found published accounts in interviews with accomplished creators and other professionals. More recently, I have started to more systematically collect data on these phenomena and have developed an initial theoretical model (discussed later in the chapter).

My initial work suggests that although not everyone has experienced creative mortification, around two thirds or more have experienced it first hand or can identify someone they know who has. Moreover, those who have experienced it have experienced it across a range of domains. Some have experienced it in more artistic domains (e.g., dance, music, art), and others have experienced it more in academic and kinesthetic domains (e.g., science, writing, math, sports). Also, some have experienced it in one particular domain of interest whereas others have experienced it across multiple domains. A key commonality across these experiences, however, is that those who have experienced creative mortification can often quickly and vividly recall how and when it occurred.

Peggy Orenstein, the accomplished journalist and author, described how upon reflecting on her prior schooling experience she was able to vividly recall, in rapid succession, several instances that resulted in her experience of creative mortification in drawing, music, and math (Orenstein, 2011):

> I recalled my beloved kindergarten teacher putting my drawing of the solar system into what was obviously the "bad" pile; being repeatedly, negatively compared to my musically gifted brother; being mocked for wrong answers as one of the few girls in eighth-grade accelerated math. (p. 4)

Creative mortification typically occurs when someone is young or in the early stages of developing their creative competence. But, it can also occur with older, more accomplished creators. Thomas Hardy, for instance, was so discouraged by the harsh criticism of his novel *Jude the Obscure* that he stopped writing novels and focused instead on writing poetry (Fitch, 1912). The creative mortification of children, however, is of primary concern. If children experience creative mortification, it can rob them of the lifelong enjoyment and the positive benefits of having creative hobbies and avocations (Richards, 2007). Moreover, creative mortification can also result in talent loss (Hong & Milgram, 2007).

Talent loss refers to the failure to realize one's potential in some given domain or aspiration. This loss not only negatively impacts the individual experiencing it but also undermines potential creative contributions that could have been made to others. The problem with talent loss is that once potential has been undermined, one never really knows what has been lost. All that remains is the unsatisfying and regretful question of "What might have been?"

Creative Mortification: An Example

A more detailed example may be helpful to illustrate some of the common features of creative mortification and serve as an anchoring example to return to throughout the remaining discussion. The following example, a vignette from the *Rhode Island Schoolmaster* (DeMunn & Snow, 1865, p. 88), illustrates several common features of creative mortification.

A child (Jane) had the aspiration to become a singer. One day, as Jane started to sing with her classmates, her teacher stopped her and asked, "Jane, what are you trying to sing? The tune sung by the old cow when she died? What a discord!" Jane stopped singing in this moment "dropped her head upon the desk, and the bitter tears ran down her cheeks" (DeMunn & Snow, 1865, p. 88). Her classmates laughed at the teacher's remark and then continued to sing without Jane. Seeing how Jane reacted, the teacher was sorry for the remark but thought Jane would soon forget about it.

However, the teacher's comments had a lingering creative mortifying effect on Jane; "the remembrance of those words would always remain with Jane, to keep her, in the future, from the vain attempt to sing" (DeMunn & Snow, 1865, p. 88). Even though Jane "cherished the idea of becoming a singer" she would no longer pursue her aspiration and, instead, chose to "bury the desire, rather than subject herself to ridicule again" (p. 88). Importantly, even though Jane's teacher felt that she would soon forget about the pain of the moment, the message that Jane received was that she did not have the ability to become a singer, "to *her* the fact that the teacher ridiculed her efforts was evidence that she could never learn" (DeMunn & Snow, 1865, p. 88).

In reviewing this anecdote, several core features of creative mortification can be identified. Specifically, the child had a creative aspiration ("... she had cherished the idea of becoming a singer"), and she was early in her development as a singer. She received negative performance-related feedback ("Jane, what are you trying to sing?...What a discord!"), and she interpreted that feedback as evidence that she was not capable of improving her singing ability ("the fact that the teacher ridiculed her efforts was evidence that she could never learn"). Jane also experienced shame ("Jane stopped singing, dropped her head upon the desk, and the bitter tears ran down her cheeks"). And, finally, the event had a lasting creative suppressing effect on her ("the remembrance of those words would always remain with Jane ... she would bury the desire, rather than subject herself to ridicule again").

Taken together, these various features of the above vignette effectively illustrate the core elements of creative mortification, but an important question remains: Why do some students experience creative mortification and others do not? One way to address this question is to compare the path of creative development with the path of creative mortification.

Elements of Creative Mortification and Development

A visual representation illustrating the bifurcation of possible trajectories of early creative aspirations (one leading to creative mortification and the other leading to continued creative development) is displayed in Figure 6.1.

As illustrated in Figure 6.1, both creative mortification and creative development share the common features of creative aspiration and negative performance-related feedback. The key point of divergence in the trajectories is how that negative performance-related feedback is delivered and,

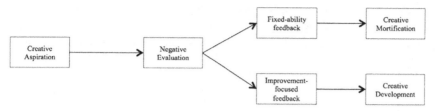

FIGURE 6.1.

in turn, subjectively interpreted by the child. As will be discussed, the way feedback is delivered can play a role in how it is interpreted and whether it will result in creative mortification or creative development. In order to understand this process, it is important to take a closer look at each of the core elements, starting with creative aspiration.

Creative Aspirations

Over the course of their childhood, children may become interested in a great many things. When children have opportunities to explore various forms of creative expression (e.g., writing, sports, drawing, science, dance), they are likely to return to those that are intrinsically motivating and participate in those activities for no other reason than they find enjoyment in doing so (Ryan & Deci, 2000). Over time and with increased opportunities to engage in these activities, the child can move from exploratory tinkering ("I like drawing") to personally identifying with the creative activity ("I am an artist"). In this way, a creative activity can eventually become part of a child's aspirational-self ("I am going to be an artist when I grow up").

Creative aspirations serve as a catalyst for developing creative potential into higher levels of creative accomplishment. Viewed from the Four-C Model of creativity (Kaufman & Beghetto, 2009), for instance, the development of creative competence starts in early life with a youngster exploring various domains and having a variety of mini-c creative experiences and insights. Over time, with repeated practice and encouragement, children's mini-c explorations can develop into personal interests and more objective forms of little-c contributions. The child will then start to identify with a specific area or domain, and the creative interest will be forged into a creative passion or aspiration. With many years of sustained and deliberate practice, the child will develop into a more accomplished creator, perhaps eventually reaching a professional (or Pro-c) level of creative accomplishment. At this level, the creative person is making a substantial contribution to a particular domain or profession. In extremely rare instances, such contributions might achieve legendary status—influencing the history of a profession or domain that extends beyond the life of the creator. In short, accomplished creators (be they Pro-c or Big-C) have their genesis in mini-c explorations that they have cultivated, over many years of deliberate practice (Ericsson, 1996), into more highly accomplished forms of creative expression (Kaufman & Beghetto, 2009).

Of course, this pattern varies somewhat by domain (e.g., artists versus scientists), and it is also possible for some creators to deviate from the developmental trajectory described above (cf., Kaufman & Beghetto, 2009). It is typically the case, however, that accomplished creators started their creative development early in life and progressed gradually in developing their creative competence. Biographies of highly accomplished scientists, for example, have highlighted a link between early hobbies that were aligned with later disciplinary pursuits and accomplishments (Simonton, 2009). Although personally identifying with one's creative aspiration is common for those who go on to develop their creative potential, it is also a precursor for those who have experienced creative mortification.

Personal Identification

Why might personally identifying with a creative aspiration serve as an antecedent to creative mortification? One reason is that identifying with a creative endeavor makes a person more vulnerable to interpreting negative performance-related feedback as a shameful indictment of the creative self (Lewis & Sullivan, 2005).

Indeed, without viewing a particular form of creative expression as an extension of the self, negative feedback may result in a temporary disappointment, but it is unlikely to have the devastating and long-lasting effect of dashing one's aspirations. Recall from the above example of Jane how she had self-identified with becoming a singer ("cherished the idea of becoming a singer"), how devastated she was from the comments of her teacher ("dropped her head on the desk, bitter tears running down her cheeks"), and how she then abandoned her creative aspiration ("buried her desire to become a singer rather than subject herself to the possibility of ridicule again").

Research on the experience of shame has provided insight into why personally identifying with a creative aspiration might serve as a precursor to creative mortification. This is because self-identification with a creative aspiration activates what has been called "self-focused attention" (Tracy & Robbins, 2004). This, in turn, can trigger damning self-appraisals following negative feedback on one's creative performance. When this happens, a person is more likely to avoid subsequent evaluative feedback opportunities in an effort to avoid pain and shame. Avoiding the risk of subsequent performance evaluations makes sense because doing so serves the protective function of buffering the person from (re)experiencing the shame and pain of the initial negative evaluation. Although this makes sense, doing so comes with the cost of also buffering oneself from opportunities to receive necessary feedback to develop one's creative competence.

To summarize, having an early creative aspiration is a common antecedent of both creative competence and creative mortification. Specifically, personally identifying with a creative aspiration not only provides motivation for those who go on to fulfill their aspirations, but it also makes youngsters more vulnerable to the experience of creative mortification. However, personal identification alone doesn't explain why some people can benefit from negative evaluative feedback and use it to develop their creative competence whereas others experience that feedback as mortifying. In order to understand how this might occur, it is important to take a closer look at how people experience performance-related feedback.

Performance-related Feedback

As has been discussed, developing one's creative competence requires many years of intense, deliberate practice (Ericsson, 1996). This involves receiving and acting on performance-related feedback. Performance-related feedback helps students identify their current strengths and limitations, set appropriately challenging goals, and focus their efforts on improvement (Bandura, 1997; Cianci, Klein, & Seijts, 2010).

Understanding how children experience performance-related feedback is the key issue on which the problem of creative mortification turns. Indeed, the initial mini-c spark of creativity that youngsters demonstrate to others can be crushed if not nurtured properly (Beghetto & Kaufman, 2007). Most educators seem to recognize this and view harshly negative feedback as potentially detrimental. What is often less obvious is that providing unwarranted praise can also stifle the development of creative competence. Creative development requires striking a balance between providing feedback that is neither too harsh nor too flattering but instead is challenging, informative, and supportive (Beghetto & Kaufman, 2007).

Recognizing this balance is one thing; achieving it when providing feedback is quite another. This is because most educators recognize that "expressing faith" in youngsters' capabilities can bolster their confidence (Bandura, 1997) and are therefore well practiced and often focused on doing so. Unfortunately, this type of praise-focused feedback is not sufficient to build and sustain youngsters' creative competence. Indeed, children who are in the early stages of developing their creative competence also need opportunities to share and test-out their mini-c expressions and receive honest, and at times negative, performance-related feedback. Importantly, negative feedback does not refer to its emotional quality (i.e., hurtful, mean spirited), but rather refers to feedback that points out errors, mistakes, and limitations of a particular performance. Such feedback is necessary for helping children refine and develop their mini-c level expressions into more accomplished creative contributions (Beghetto, 2007b).

Providing too much support (through excessive praise for mediocre performance, unchallenging tasks, and repeatedly offering unsolicited help) can have a damaging effect on children's motivation and competence development (Bandura, 1997; Beghetto & Kaufman, 2007). Moreover, as Bandura (1997) has explained, "Unrealistic boosts in efficacy are readily disconfirmed by disappointing results of one's actions. By acting on highly inflated self-beliefs, one quickly finds out what one cannot do" (p. 104).

To summarize, in addition to providing positive recognition of what youngsters have already accomplished, educators also need to provide the kind of negative performance-related feedback that can help students recognize how they might further develop their competence. In order to do so, educators need to understand under what circumstances such feedback might be more or less likely to lead to an experience of creative mortification. One way to provide insight into this issue is to view the experience of negative-performance feedback through the lens of two related psychological phenomena: self-theories of competence and self-conscious emotions.

Self-theories of Competence

A key factor in predicting how a child will respond to negative performance-evaluative feedback has to do with how they subjectively interpret that feedback. Put simply: how students interpret negative evaluative feedback—whether it signifies that their creative ability is fixed versus capable of growth (Dweck, 2000)—influences how they will respond to that feedback.

The research of Carol Dweck and her colleagues has consistently demonstrated how one's self-theories or "mindset" about ability (i.e., viewing ability as a fixed "entity" or an "incremental" process of growth) can play a critical role in determining whether a person will be more likely to respond to negative evaluative feedback in an adverse (versus more advantageous) manner.

Although children may already have a general belief about the nature of their creative ability (e.g., that it is fixed, that it can change, or unsure), what is most important for the present discussion is that their belief can be influenced by how the feedback is delivered to them in a particular moment. Even subtle linguistic cues can have this influence. Moreover, and somewhat ironically, even positive praise that speaks to fixed ability versus effort can have a detrimental impact.

Findings from a recent study of preschool age children (Cimpian, Arce, Markman, & Dweck, 2007), for instance, indicate that children who acted out a part as a puppet and received ability-related praise from a teacher-puppet ("You are a good drawer") were significantly more likely to feel demoralized, denigrate their ability, feel sad, and avoid drawing when criticized by the teacher-puppet for making mistakes as compared to children who received more task-specific praise ("You did a good job drawing"). This is because ability-related feedback cultivates a self-belief that success and mistakes are the result of fixed ability, whereas more task-specific feedback implies that ability is not fixed and that mistakes can be repaired and improved upon with more effort.

When providing negative evaluative feedback, how it is said and, most importantly, how it is interpreted will help determine whether children believe that their creative ability is fixed or capable of growth. As Baron (1988) has noted, "it is not the delivery of negative feedback, per se, that produces such effects; rather, the manner in which such information is conveyed" (p. 205). Thus, the way feedback is presented—specifically whether or not it signifies to the recipient that improvement is possible—will help determine whether a child's creative competence will be stifled or supported.

Returning to the above example of Jane, the aspiring singer, it was her interpretation that she would never improve as a singer that resulted in her avoiding any future "vain attempt to sing" (DeMunn & Snow, 1865). Ability-related feedback coupled with personally identifying with the creative expression magnifies the intensity of how that feedback is heard and the consequence of that feedback.

Consider, for example, the experience of Ana Castillo. Castillo is a highly accomplished creative writer and social activist; however, when she was a child she held a passion for both drawing and writing, "I wrote poetry and wrote stories and drew on whatever I could, painted on whatever I could, anything, any piece of paper that was around" (Saeta, 1997, par. 6). By college age Castillo decided she wanted to be a professional visual artist. Castillo goes on to explain that she experienced such harsh discouragement in college that she ultimately stopped drawing and painting: "By the time I was finishing my B.A....I was really convinced that I had no talent. I couldn't draw and I had no right to be painting. And I couldn't draw anymore—I literally did not draw or paint anymore" (Saeta, 1997, par. 6).

Castillo's last statement signifies what is meant by the experience of creative mortification: discouragement resulting in the indefinite suspension of creative expression. Castillo's aspiration to be a visual artist had its roots in her early personal engagement with and enjoyment of drawing and painting. This artistic aspiration died as a result of the harsh devaluate experience she had at the university.

To summarize, when children receive negative, fixed-ability feedback on their creative aspirations (e.g., "Your torso is too small to be a gymnast") they are likely to believe there is nothing they can do to improve. Moreover, because they self-identify with this aspiration, negative ability-related feedback is likely to be interpreted as a shameful indictment of the creative self (Lewis & Sullivan, 2005).

Consequently, not only do youngsters believe that they can't improve but they also have an accompanying negative emotional experience associated with the event. In order to further understand how experiencing negative emotions (like shame) can result in creative mortification, it is important to take a brief look at a particular type of emotion, called self-conscious evaluative emotions.

Self-conscious Evaluative Emotions

Self-conscious evaluative emotions are a special class of emotions, different from the basic emotions of, for instance, happiness and sadness. Specifically, self-conscious evaluative emotions provide the "emotional backdrop" (Lewis & Sullivan, 2005) for the development of competence and include pride, shame, guilt, and embarrassment. The experience of these emotions plays an important role in determining whether students will be motivated to strive harder, put forth sustained effort, and overcome challenges or avoid and give-up on a particular pursuit.

Self-conscious emotions develop as early as two years of age and enable people to interpret and take responsibility for success and failure (Lewis & Sullivan, 2005). Moreover, self-conscious emotions are thought to occur any time someone attributes an event or outcome to internal causes (Lewis & Sullivan, 2005; Tracy & Robbins, 2006). More specifically, if that event or outcome is perceived to be negative, and the child views that outcome as resulting from some self-limitation, then the child is likely to experience the self-conscious emotion of shame or guilt (Tracy & Robbins, 2006).

The experience of such emotions plays an important role in determining whether a child will be motivated to develop his or her competence or become avoidant of such opportunities. Experiencing the negative emotion of shame, as Lewis & Sullivan (2005) have explained, will likely result in the child becoming avoidant of the people or circumstances that elicited that emotion. The experience of shame also leads to self-condemnation—a belief that the shaming experience happened because "I am bad." Moreover, as Lewis & Sullivan (2005) have explained, "this type of total self-focus is particularly damaging, because there is no way out" (p. 189). Consequently, when children feel that there is no way to improve their abilities, they are likely to lose the motivation to engage in and further develop their creative aspirations.

Understanding the combination of self-conscious emotions (specifically, shame) and self theories about ability (specifically, fixed versus growth beliefs) can help explain and predict whether negative evaluative feedback will have a mortifying or edifying impact on the development and attainment of a youngster's creative aspiration. In an effort to bring all these elements together, it may be helpful to provide a concluding example of how negative feedback can result in the development of creative competence.

Negative Feedback and Creative Development

As has been discussed, negative feedback does not necessarily lead to creative mortification. Negative evaluative feedback can provide important and necessary information to students on how they can improve their creative competence. The highly accomplished composer Steven Sondheim serves as an important example.

In a recent interview on the book discussion program *Bookworm* (Alvarez & Howard, 2010), Sondheim explained a key formative experience he had with his mentor Oscar Hammerstein. Sondheim was fifteen years old at the time and had written a school show and submitted it to Hammerstein for feedback. Sondheim asked Hammerstein to treat the show as if he did not know he wrote it, saying, "Pretend you don't know me and it had just crossed your desk." In response, Hammerstein said, "well in that case I have to tell you it is the worst thing I have ever read" (Alvarez & Howard, 2010).

Hammerstein's feedback represents a key evaluative micromoment. If, for example, the interaction stopped at this moment, it is unclear how Sondheim would have interpreted this seemingly harsh evaluation. There is little doubt that this would be difficult to hear for any young, aspiring songwriter. Moreover, given what we know from prior research on self-conscious evaluative emotions and self-theories, it is quite possible that if Hammerstein's feedback had stopped at this point, then Sondheim may have quite understandably internalized this feedback, viewing it as a shameful indictment of his creative abilities, and perhaps given up on writing show tunes.

Fortunately, Hammerstein went well beyond this rather harsh evaluation and explained how Sondheim could improve it. Specifically, as Sondheim explains, "He treated me like an adult and he did it as an encouragement" (Alvarez & Howard, 2010). Hammerstein provided detailed, improvement-focused feedback on how the songs were structured, the rhyme and scene construction, and how the characters evolved and also pointed out inconsistencies. As Sondheim notes, "He went through it page by page," and even though they did not get all the way through it, Sondheim explains that he "probably learned more about song writing for theatre that afternoon than most writers probably learn in a lifetime" (Alvarez & Howard, 2010).

This example illustrates just how important informative, improvement-oriented feedback can be. Taking the time to point out what specifically is wrong and how it can be improved is the hallmark of effective instructional feedback (Black & Wiliam, 1998). Moreover, and most important with respect to creative mortification, doing so also signals to the student receiving the feedback that the limitation is not due to a fixed ability that can't be changed, but can be improved with subsequent effort. This alters the entire emotional tone and lasting impact of the experience—changing it from a potentially devastating experience of shame to a disappointment that, with support, can fuel subsequent improvement and effort. This is evident in how Sondheim responded to the follow-up question asked by the interviewer (Alvarez & Howard, 2010):

Interviewer: "It must have been crushing...how quickly were you able to adapt?"

Sondheim: "Oh, in five minutes because it was so fascinating listening to him talk about it and you know I knew he loved me or at least liked me at the very least... it was a disappointment not a hurt."

In this way, negative, even seemingly harsh, feedback does not always have a mortifying effect on the development of creative potential. If delivered in such a way that youngsters can perceive it as informative and signifying the possibility of improvement, negative feedback can serve to develop and edify one's developing creative competence.

To summarize, the difference between Sondheim's experience of negative performance-related feedback and Jane's experience is in how the feedback was delivered and experienced. For Jane, negative feedback was experienced as a shameful indictment of her creative self—communicating a fixed and unalterable limitation in her singing ability. Conversely, Sondheim experienced negative feedback as an indication that he had much more work to do to become an accomplished writer of show tunes—communicating a limitation that could be remedied through guidance and subsequent effort.

The key turning point, then, is in how negative feedback is delivered and experienced. The important and simple take-away from all of this for teachers is: When providing feedback to students, be sure to point out what they did well and how specifically they might improve—stressing that improvement is possible with subsequent effort and guidance. Of course, simply providing improvement-oriented feedback will not somehow magically turn mini-c children into eminent Big-C creators. Still, what it can do is ensure that all students have an opportunity to learn how to improve and enjoy creative expression—even if that creative expression remains at the little-c level.

CONCLUDING THOUGHTS

The development of creative potential can sometimes be put in peril as a result of the everyday evaluative interactions in the classroom. The purpose of this chapter was to highlight a particularly severe form of creative suppression: creative mortification. Creative mortification can result from how students experience negative performance-related feedback. I presented several examples of creative mortification and an initial, theoretical model that serves to highlight the key elements of creative mortification. Although the model needs (and is currently undergoing) additional empirical testing and refinement, it can still serve as a useful outline of the process of creative mortification. Important for educators to keep in mind is that although creative mortification is possible in most any classroom or educational setting, it is not inevitable.

The best way for educators to address the problems associated with this form of creative suppression is to try to prevent it from happening in the first place. As has been discussed throughout this chapter, educators (be they teachers, parents, or coaches) play a central role in whether students will experience negative performance-related feedback as mortifying or edifying. Much depends on how that feedback is delivered and received. Specifically, if students interpret negative feedback as evidence of a fixed, limited ability, then they will be more at risk of experiencing creative mortification than if educators take the additional step of stressing how students might improve through continued effort and deliberate practice.

This requires monitoring how students are interpreting negative performance-related feedback and also making sure that when providing positive (or praise-oriented) feedback, the focus is on competence resulting from putting forth effort rather than on fixed ability (see Dweck, 2000). Doing so is much easier said than done because the types of praise-related statements that many people have learned typically focus on ability ("You are so smart!" or "You're the best gymnast!") rather than focusing on effort ("Wow, you've clearly put a lot of thought into that paper!" or "Nice job. I can tell that you've been practicing your handstands!")

Finally, we would all do well to practice what might be called *mindfulness in the micromoments of evaluation* so that a seemingly throwaway or rushed "off-the-cuff" comment doesn't inadvertently result in the stifling of a child's creative potential. One way to do so is to be mindful of whether and how the everyday interactions and features of the classroom environment are supportive of creative expression. Ideas for how to think about and establish creative supportive contexts will be discussed in the next chapter.

PART III

REALIZING THE CREATIVE POTENTIAL OF THE CLASSROOM

CHAPTER 7

TOWARD CREATIVITY CONDUCIVE CLASSROOM ENVIRONMENTS

The problem is we seldom stop to notice what just happened. Without such reflection, we go blindly on our way... creating more unintended consequences... It's amazing to me how much we do, but how little time we spend reflecting on what we just did.

—Wheatley, 2007, p. 208

Teaching is a blend of highly planned and improvised behavior (Sawyer, 2011). This unique and somewhat paradoxical blend of behaviors occurs under time and curricular constraints. This makes it difficult for teachers to stop and notice what just happened, what was just done, and the unintended consequences of one's instructional actions. However, without attending to how students experience the policies, practices, and procedures of the everyday classroom, teachers can inadvertently and unknowingly suppress creativity. Teachers who successfully teach for creativity are therefore mindful of the influences of the classroom environment and frequently monitor how students experience that environment.

Killing Ideas Softly? The Promise and Perils of Creativity in the Classroom, pages 103–117.

Creativity researchers have documented how the social environment can impact creativity (Amabile, 1996). Much of this research has been conducted in organizations and work environments (Amabile, Conti, Coon, Lazenby, & Herron, 1996; Hunter, Bedell, & Mumford, 2007), but there has also been an active and ongoing line of research conducted in classroom settings (Hennessey, 2010a). Understanding findings from this line of research can help teachers develop a better understanding of how they might establish a classroom environment more conducive to creativity.

The goal of this chapter is to demonstrate that students' experience of the classroom context matters. The chapter is organized in two parts. The first part highlights the importance of being aware of the unintended consequences communicated by instructional practices and actions. Some of these unintended consequences result from subtle messages communicated in the everyday classroom. Others result from teachers' intended efforts to motivate students. The second part of the chapter is focused on what teachers can do to cultivate a classroom more conducive to the development of students' creative competence—specifically, protecting students' intrinsic motivation, using extrinsic motivators more effectively, and cultivating students' healthy self-beliefs.

TOWARD NOTICING WHAT JUST HAPPENED

Subject matter teaching typically involves identifying goals and outcomes in advance of teaching them to students. This helps teachers ensure that lessons stay focused and that students are presented with opportunities to learn the academic subject matter that teachers are responsible to teach. The sometimes hidden cost of this goal-directed and outcome-based aspect of teaching is that a variety of problematic and often unintended mini-messages can be communicated to students along the way.

Unintended mini-messages of the everyday classroom

Unintended mini-messages are subtle motivational messages sent by everyday classroom practices, policies, and procedures that impact students' willingness to engage in learning activities and creative expression. Teachers are often unaware that these messages are being sent and how students are experiencing these messages. What might mini-messages look like in the flow of the everyday classroom?

Unintended Mini-messages: An example

An example of a mini-message is illustrated in the sixth grade hypothesis lesson (Hannah & Abate, 1995) introduced in Chapter 5. The lesson opens with the teacher encouraging students to share their conceptions of a hypothesis. After several students offer suggestions, one student, Rob, offers that a hypothesis is "a kind of idea." The teacher then indicates that Rob has the answer and then briefly elaborates on this definition. Prior to transitioning to a small group hypothesis testing activity, the teacher spends a few moments introducing the activity and inviting students to share their ideas about the activity before they begin.

> *Teacher:* Your job for the next five minutes or so…and that's all your gonna get… is to come up with a hypothesis. Now, what are you coming up with a hypothesis about? Anyone have a hypothesis about what your hypothesis is gonna be about? [Smiling, raising her eyebrows, and motioning her hands to a box of onions on the window ledge at the front of the classroom].
>
> *Teacher:* Stacy?
>
> *Stacy:* [Whose view of the onion box is obstructed by other students but who can see a turkey on a bulletin board in the direction the teacher is motioning] Thanksgiving?
>
> *Teacher:* Could be Thanksgiving, because Thanksgiving is coming. Roxanne?
>
> *Roxanne:* [Who can see the box of onions on the window ledge] Onions?
>
> *Teacher:* Onions! Roxanne was thinking!

The teacher's seemingly benign response, "Roxanne was thinking" can unintentionally communicate to other students—who were also sharing ideas—that they were somehow not thinking. There are several potential consequences that can result from such a message. One consequence is the reinforcement of the *intellectual hide-n-seek* pattern of talk introduced in Chapter 5. That is, respond to the teacher only if you know the answer the teacher wants to hear. Another related consequence students might learn is that it is risky to share one's own ideas. Even when invited to do so. Some students, therefore, might learn that it simply is not worth the risk to share their own ideas.

This example illustrates a key theme of this chapter. Specifically, seemingly throwaway comments and other everyday features of the classroom can have an unintended impact on students' willingness to share their own ideas. Consequently, students' creative potential is suppressed because they miss out on opportunities to test-out and refine their mini-c ideas.

In addition to the unintended mini-messages of the everyday classroom, there are also motivational mini-messages of the classroom that communicate to students the opposite of what was intended. Indeed, as will be discussed in the next section, sometimes teachers' efforts to motivate students to engage and be creative can actually stifle students' creative expression.

Motivational Mini-Messages

A reality of K–12 teaching is that teachers are responsible for teaching subject matter that may not be inherently interesting to students (Ryan & Deci, 2000). When confronted with such situations, teachers commonly try a variety of strategies in an effort to persuade or motivate (i.e., literally "move") students to engage with subject matter.

One way to try to motivate students is to let them know that those who do the best or most creative work will be rewarded in some way (e.g., display their work on the classroom walls, select a prize from the class treasure box). Another way to try to motivate students to engage in the task and put forth creative effort is to let them know that their work will be evaluated. Yet another way is to use competitions or other social comparisons. Although these types of extrinsic motivators can drive some students to strive and get the work done, they can also have an unintended and opposite effect (Hennessey, 2010a). The relationship between motivation and creativity can be somewhat counterintuitive. It is therefore important to take a closer look at how teachers' efforts to motivate students can send mini-messages that have an unintended impact on students' motivation and creativity.

Example 1: Best Work Wall

Let's take a closer look at the common practice of displaying only the "best" work on the classroom walls. Teachers sometimes use this strategy in an effort to motivate their students to work hard and, in turn, enjoy the rewards of social recognition. One can imagine hearing a teacher explaining to students that those who develop the best and most creative work (be it a poem, drawing, short story) will have the opportunity to have their work displayed on the "best work wall." Although it is possible for such practices to motivate some students to strive to take intellectual risks and express their creativity, there is compelling evidence to suggest that for many other students it can have the directly opposite effect. Why might this be the case?

One reason is that some students might feel that they have no chance of making it on the best work wall and therefore see no point in trying. But this only explains why some students' motivation might be undermined; why might it be the case that such a practice can have a much broader negative impact? The reason is a bit subtler and has to do with the message being sent to students regarding the rationale or basis for why they should engage in the assigned task.

Motivation is not simply a matter of quantity (i.e., some students having more or less motivation); there are also different types of motivation that concern the "why of action" (Ryan & Deci, 2000). At the most basic level of distinction, there are internal reasons (e.g., enjoyment, satisfaction, interest) referred to as intrinsic motivation and external reasons (e.g., please others, obtain rewards, avoid pain or punishment) referred to as extrinsic motivation (Ryan & Deci, 2000). These reasons for action are communicated to students in the way teachers organize, describe, and encourage participation in various learning activities and tasks.

Returning to the best work wall example, the most salient reason for engaging in the assigned task and working hard is the reward of social recognition. In short, students are working for an expected reward. Expected rewards can direct students' motivation away from the inherent interest and natural enjoyment found in a particular task (e.g., the interest and enjoyment that comes from personal expression found in writing poetry, drawing pictures) and toward an external reason (i.e., social recognition). The quality of one's experience and the performance outcomes of that experience can be very different when one is behaving for external reasons as compared to internal reasons (Ryan & Deci, 2000).

With respect to the impact that this can have on creativity, a longstanding program of research has rather convincingly demonstrated the detrimental effects that expected reward can have on students' intrinsic motivation and, in turn, creative expression (Amabile, 1996; Hennessey, 2010a). One of the earliest studies to highlight this detrimental effect on creativity was conducted by Kruglanski, Friedman, and Zeevi (1971). The results of this study demonstrated how being promised a reward could lower high school students' enjoyment and creativity as compared to students who performed the task without having the expectation of receiving a reward.

Over the past several decades, numerous researchers have consistently demonstrated a negative relationship between reward expectations and creativity—including receiving a reward prior to engaging in the task (see Amabile, Hennessey, & Grossman, 1986). Hennessey (2010b), for instance, has summarized the results of these studies by explaining that across "hundreds of published investigations" the same basic finding has been demonstrated. Specifically, "the promise of a reward made contingent on task engagement often serves to undermine intrinsic task motivation and qualitative aspects of performance, including creativity" (p. 345). Moreover, as Hennessey notes, "This effect is so robust that it has been found to occur across a wide age range with everyone from preschoolers to seasoned business professionals" (p. 345).

When interpreting these results, it is important to keep in mind that these studies point to the increased likelihood of this happening. Using rewards to motivate students will not diminish creativity for every student, in every setting, or every time. Some students can and will be motivated by rewards (Amabile, 1996; Eisenberger & Cameron, 1998; Eisenberger & Shanock, 2003). The potential detrimental effect of rewards on creativity, however, warrants caution in how teachers use rewards.

The key is for teachers to recognize that the use of rewards to try to motivate engagement and performance can have the unanticipated outcome of undermining students' interest, enjoyment, and creative performance. As such, teachers should use rewards judiciously. When teachers choose to use rewards, they should also monitor how those rewards are impacting students' intrinsic interest. A clear sign that rewards are having a negative impact on students' intrinsic interest would be when a child who enjoys drawing and typically adds illustrations to his stories starts asking, "What will I get if I add drawings to my story?"

In addition to rewards, there are various other common features of typical classroom activities and assignments that can have a similar adverse effect. These are discussed in the example that follows.

Example 2: Math Cars

Imagine a third grade teacher who wants to make individual math practice more enjoyable and engaging. She comes up with a clever racetrack activity that will serve as the backdrop for completing math practice worksheets. Specifically, in an attempt to engage and motivate her students when working on practice problems, she has students personalize paper cutouts of racecars that will serve as markers of progress during math class. Each student is asked to put his or her name on the car, color it, and hang it on the racetrack above the chalkboard for everyone to see. The teacher hands students a worksheet of practice problems. She announces that for each student who correctly answers the questions on the worksheet in the allotted time, his or her math car will move one step toward the finish line.

Although the structure of this activity is intended to make practice exercises in math more enjoyable and engaging, it can actually have the exact opposite impact on student interest and creativity. What is most problematic about this activity is that it makes several extrinsic features of the task highly salient to students: Quick completion is more important than taking the time to understand and experiment with different ways of solving a problem, mistakes should be avoided, and only the quickest students' cars will move.

Some students undoubtedly will have difficulty completing the worksheet in the allotted time. For those students whose cars have not yet moved, they are reminded in a very public way that they are not as smart, quick, or capable as their peers. Moreover, it is not inconceivable to imagine how otherwise capable students might feel pressured by the highly visible nature of their progress and start doubting their ability to succeed in math. This, in turn, could lead to their adoption of an avoidant attitude toward math.

Avoidant motivational orientations are, in part, influenced by classroom structures (like the math car motivational strategy) and can result in students adopting the primary motivational goal of wanting to avoid looking incompetent in the eyes of their teachers and peers (Midgley, 2002). Students who want to avoid looking incompetent may resort to a wide range of problematic behaviors including refusing to try, cheating, and even becoming disruptive (Maehr & Midgley, 1996; Midgley, 2002).

In addition to the possibility of students adopting an avoidant motivational orientation, several core aspects of the math car activity can have a detrimental impact on student interest and creativity. Those potentially detrimental aspects include externally imposed time constraints, competitive social-comparison, and the expectation of evaluation. With respect to imposed time constraints, Amabile and her colleagues (Amabile, DeJong, & Lepper 1976) demonstrated that deadlines for completing a word game task had an adverse effect on participants' intrinsic interest (as compared to participants who finished the task but did not face such deadlines). Similar detrimental effects on motivation and creativity have been linked to tasks that emphasize competition and expected evaluations (Amabile, 1979, 1982; Amabile, Goldfarb, & Brackfield, 1990).

Indeed, one of the most problematic aspects of the math car activity is that it highlights social comparison among students. Concerns about comparisons to others and evaluation pressures can cause anxiety that undermines students' willingness and capacity for creative expression (Collins & Amabile, 1999; Runco, 2003; Tighe, Picariello, & Amabile, 2003). This is particularly problematic when comparisons are made in a highly visible fashion (e.g., displaying the progress of math cars on the front chalkboard).

Taken together, the core features of the math car activity—social comparison, time constraints, evaluation, and expected reward—represent a potentially deadly combination of extrinsic motivators and constraints. As Hennessey (2010b) has explained, "the expectation that one's work will be judged and compared...may well be the most deleterious extrinsic constraint of all...because...competition often combines aspects of other 'killers' of motivation and creativity, including expected reward and expected evaluation" (p. 348).

Finally, the math car activity also communicates to students the importance of quickly converging on correct answers (as this is the only way students' math cars can advance toward the finish line). As a result, students can experience the math car activity, somewhat ironically, as more test-like (i.e., focus on ability to arrive at correct answers) rather than game-like (i.e., practice your skills, mistakes are okay). When this happens, students are less likely to take the types of intellectual risks that are supportive of meaningful learning and creativity.

Clifford and Chou (1991), for instance, found that when Taiwanese fourth graders were told they were playing a game ("play a game to practice your thinking skills") versus told to demonstrate their ability on a school-like task ("take a test to show how good your thinking skills are"), students who believed they were engaged in a game were significantly more likely to take intellectual risks than students who believed they were engaged in a test-like task.

Students who are willing to take intellectual risks (e.g., sharing novel ideas and insights, raising new questions, and attempting to do and try new things) have a better chance of developing their academic and creative proficiency (Beghetto, 2009a). However, when the task environment of the classroom undermines students' interest and discourages intellectual risk-taking, students are much less likely to take the risks necessary for sharing and developing their mini-c ideas because they fear making mistakes, appearing inferior, or looking less competent in comparison to their peers (Beghetto, 2009a; Dweck, 2000; Midgley, 2002).

To summarize, the math car activity and best work wall are examples of well-intended motivational strategies that can send problematic mini-messages that negatively impact students' motivation and creativity. As such, they serve to illustrate Amabile's (1996) Intrinsic Motivation Principle of Creativity. This principle asserts that intrinsic motivation is typically conducive to creativity, whereas extrinsic motivators and extrinsic task constraints typically have an adverse effect on creativity (Hennessey, 2010b). Specifically, extrinsic motivators (e.g., task-contingent rewards) and constraints in the social environment (e.g., time limits, expected evaluation, social comparison) can serve to orient one's motivation away from internal reasons for engaging in the task and toward external reasons. This shift in motivational orientation can, in turn, have an adverse impact on interest, intellectual risk taking, and creativity.

Again, this is not to say that extrinsic motivators should never be used. Rather, the point to remember is that our best intentions to motivate students can sometimes yield unexpected and opposite results. It is therefore important to try to understand how students experience the motivational messages being sent in the learning environment. By paying attention to how students are experiencing classroom routines, procedures, and tasks, teachers can be in a better position to foster student learning and creativity. So, the question is not whether features of the classroom environment impact students' motivation and creativity, but rather: How can teachers cultivate a creativity supportive context in the day-to-day classroom? This question is addressed in the remainder of this chapter.

CULTIVATING A CREATIVITY CONDUCIVE ENVIRONMENT

There are several things teachers can do to cultivate a classroom environment conducive to creativity. These include ways to protect students' intrinsic motivation, using extrinsic motivators more effectively, and cultivating healthy self-beliefs about creativity. Each is discussed in the sections that follow.

Protecting Students' Intrinsic Motivation

Given the link between intrinsic interests and creativity (Hennessey, 2010b), it would be ideal if classrooms were filled with intrinsically motivating experiences and activities, but as any teacher knows, this is more of an aspirational than attainable goal. Although a teacher may be able to develop activities and learning experiences that are intrinsically interesting to some students some of the time, it is much more difficult (if not impossible) for a teacher to consistently develop and incorporate learning experiences and activities that are intrinsically interesting to all students all of the time (Ryan & Deci, 2000). So what is a teacher to do?

Extrinsic motivators are an everyday part of life. It is therefore not surprising that most schools and classrooms intentionally use such motivators to engage students and keep them on track. As such, trying to remove extrinsic motivators from schools and classrooms is not a wise or feasible endeavor. Instead of trying to remove extrinsic motivators, a more fruitful effort would be to try to minimize their potentially negative effect. Fortunately, researches have explored ways of doing so and have yielded important insights that teachers can use in their own classrooms.

Beth Hennessey and her colleagues, for instance, have examined whether students might be taught how to protect their intrinsic motivation and creativity from the potential negative effects of extrinsic motivation (Hennessey, 2010b). These researchers used a medical metaphor of immunization as a way of thinking about how this might be done. To explore whether this was possible, Hennessey and her colleagues developed training videos that students watched to vicariously learn how to focus on the intrinsic features of an assigned task. Specifically, students watched videos of age-related peers talking about the intrinsically appealing features of tasks. Results of this work, although somewhat mixed (see Gerrard, Poteat, & Ironsmith, 1996), have provided evidence that students can learn how to minimize the perceived importance of extrinsic motivators and focus instead on the intrinsically motivating (i.e., interesting, fun, and exciting) aspects of tasks (Hennesey, 2010b).

The following suggestions can help teachers develop ideas for how they might protect their students' intrinsic motivation and creativity from the potentially negative effects of extrinsic features of the classroom (adapted from Hennessey, 2010a, p. 345):

- *Allow students to take control of their own learning.* Try to create a classroom atmosphere that allows students to feel in control of their learning process. Avoid trying to motivate students through coercion (e.g., "You need to do this or you will fail") and contingencies (e.g., "Complete this assignment and then you'll get free time"). Instead, provide students with opportunities to pursue their own interests so that they can develop a sense of self-initiation and direction in their learning. Doing so will help students recognize that their interests and mini-c ideas can serve as the origins of their learning, rather than feeling like "pawns" in someone else's learning goals and agenda.

- *Monitor the use of extrinsic motivators.* Occasionally review and reflect on the types of incentives that are being used in the school and classroom to motivate students. Am I using too many extrinsic motivators? How might I counter-balance my use of extrinsic motivators with more intrinsically interesting and engaging options and tasks? How might I help students focus on the intrinsically enjoyable and personally meaningful aspects of a particular learning task?

- *Identify and incorporate student interests.* Learn about your students' interests and develop opportunities for incorporating those interests in learning activities and assignments. In cases where students do find lessons and tasks interesting, be careful in how extrinsic motivators are used (e.g., try to limit the use of tangible rewards), minimize surveillance and evaluative pressures placed on students, and try to avoid situations in which student progress is compared to the progress of other students (focus instead on comparing current student progress with the student's own prior progress).

- *Encourage intrinsic engagement.* Encourage students to take reasonable risks, try things out, challenge themselves, and take pride in the effort they put into their learning tasks and assignments.

The above suggestions can go a long way in helping teachers support and protect students' inherent interest and, in turn, students' willingness to engage in creative learning and problem solving. In addition to the above suggestions for including and focusing on intrinsic motivation in the classroom, there are ways that teachers can use extrinsic motivators more effectively. The following section offers insights and practical strategies for working more effectively with extrinsic motivators.

Using Extrinsic Motivators More Effectively

Motivational researchers (e.g., Hennessey, 2010a; Reeve, 2009; Ryan & Deci, 2000) have demonstrated that teachers can learn how to use extrinsic motivators more effectively. The key is to understand how to use extrinsic motivators in a way that supports students' experience of autonomy (i.e., the endorsement and personal valuing of learning tasks and goals) rather than students' experience of external control (i.e., viewing learning tasks and goals as externally imposed and of little personal value).

Autonomy, in the context of the classroom, refers to students endorsing the value of learning tasks and being able to make conscious choices or decisions about those tasks (Reeve, 2009). Autonomy is undermined when students experience assigned learning tasks as controlling (e.g., feeling pressured by their teachers), conflicting (e.g., at odds with what students value or endorse), or coerced (e.g., feeling like they must complete an assignment to avoid guilt or punishment, rather than because it has meaning or value). In short, the experience of autonomy pertains to students' ability to identify with, endorse, internalize, and value the classroom activities, learning goals, and assignments.

Supporting students autonomy is a key way to motivate students to engage with learning activities, tasks, and assignments that they otherwise do not find inherently interesting or intrinsically motivating. The following suggestions provide teachers with ideas for how they might better support students' autonomy in the classroom (adapted from Ryan & Deci, 2006; and Reeve, 2009, pp. 160–162).

- *Provide students with meaningful options and choices.* One way teachers can do this is by providing options to students on the types of tasks they can complete and even how they might complete them (e.g., "Pick three from the following list," "Come up with your own way to..."). Doing so can increase the chances that students will be able to endorse the task (Reeve, 2009). Importantly, it's not simply the total number of options provided, but how students experience those options. As Ryan and Deci (2006) have clarified "One can have many options and not feel autonomy, but instead feel overwhelmed and resentful at the effort entailed in the decision making...one could have only one option...and yet feel quite autonomous so long as one truly endorses that option" (p. 1577). Teachers who effectively support student autonomy, therefore, need to be cognizant of providing options and how students experience those options.
- *Recognize and incorporate students' perspectives.* An autonomy supportive approach strikes a balance between the teacher's responsibility to direct instruction and being responsive to students' experiences and perspectives. Doing so requires that teachers take time to listen to their students and, when appropriate, integrate students' perspectives into the lessons, activities, and tasks of the classroom. When teachers incorporate students' perspectives into the flow of instruction, as Reeve (2009) has explained, "teachers become both more willing and able to create classroom conditions in which students' autonomous motivations align with their classroom activity" (p. 162). Students, consequently, will be more likely to endorse the learning activities, tasks, and experiences created by their teachers.
- *Provide reasons for requests.* When teachers make instructional requests of students—particularly when students do not feel those requests are inherently interesting—teachers can increase the chances that

students endorse such requests if an explanation or rationale is provided for the request (Reeve, 2009). A student, for example, is more likely to experience a teacher's request to revise an essay as supportive if the request is accompanied by a rationale that the student can endorse ("...because you want to submit it to the local newspaper, and it needs a bit more work before it is ready") as compared to a request that is accompanied by an ultimatum (e.g., "Revise it or you fail the assignment") or accompanied by guilt-inducing language (e.g., "You have to revise it before you send it in to the newspaper or you will embarrass me, yourself, and this entire school"). Being aware of how one communicates requests and how students might experience such requests can help support students' autonomy.

• *Welcome students' thoughts, feelings, and actions.* An autonomy supportive classroom is one that welcomes and respects students' thoughts, feelings, and actions—including students' negative emotions (Reeve, 2009). Autonomy supportive teachers recognize that students will respond in various ways to what they are learning and, therefore, anticipate and work with these various responses rather than pressure or coerce students to think, feel, and act in certain ways. A supportive teacher responding to a student who is frustrated by being asked to redo an assignment might respond by acknowledging the student's frustration ("I can see that you are frustrated and understand why you don't want to redo this assignment...) rather than simply dismissing the student's frustration out-of-hand (e.g., "Stop your complaining and just do it!"). By demonstrating encouragement, patience, and taking the few extra moments to listen to and treat student complaints as valid, teachers can ensure that students experience their instructional efforts as supportive (Reeve, 2009).

To summarize, teachers can support autonomy by allowing students to take control of their own learning, monitoring and minimizing the use of extrinsic motivators, incorporating student interests and perspectives, providing students with meaningful options and choices, providing reasons for instructional requests, and welcoming students' thoughts, feelings, and actions. By doing so, teachers can help create the kind of motivational environment that is not only supportive of creativity but a wide range of positive motivational and learning outcomes, including intrinsic motivation, self-determination, curiosity, engagement, positive feelings, attendance, positive self-worth, optimal challenge seeking, deep understanding, self-regulated learning, better academic performance, and general wellbeing and satisfaction (see Hennessey, 2010b; Ryan & Deci, 2000; and Reeve, 2009).

On the surface, teachers may feel like it is a daunting task to monitor the motivational experiences of their students, particularly when faced with a class of thirty or more students. Indeed, it is not possible for teachers to monitor how every student is experiencing every task at every moment. Still, teachers can make great strides in supporting students' autonomy, intrinsic motivation, and creative expression by being aware of the above guidelines and suggestions. Moreover, teachers can also take positive steps toward developing students' creative competence by cultivating students' healthy self-beliefs about their creative ability and willingness to take intellectual risks. The importance of cultivating such beliefs and suggestions for doing so are discussed in the section that follows.

Cultivating Students' Healthy Self-Beliefs

The development of creative potential starts with students having the confidence and willingness to share their ideas. Students who otherwise have the ability to demonstrate their creativity, but do not believe they are capable of doing so, likely will choose to take a safer path, reproduce what has already been done, and focus their creative energy elsewhere. In this way, students' beliefs about their creative ability and willingness to take risks play an important role in determining whether student creativity will be expressed and developed in the classroom.

Given the role that students' self-beliefs play in the development of students' creative potential, it is particularly important that teachers understand the nature of this role. Part of understanding the role of self-beliefs is to recognize that such beliefs are susceptible to bias and inaccuracy (Beghetto, Kaufman, & Baxter, 2011; Dunning, Health, & Suls, 2004). Consequently, self-beliefs should not be viewed as an expression of creativity itself, but rather as a means for augmenting student creativity. In this way, students' self-beliefs represent "creativity enhancers" that serve to reinforce students' confidence and increase the chances that students will share and, in turn, develop their creative potential into creative achievement.

Two beliefs that can play an important role in enhancing student creativity are *creative self-efficacy* and *intellectual risk-taking*. Creative self-efficacy refers to a self-judgment of one's imaginative ability and perceived competence in generating novel and adaptive ideas, solutions, and behaviors (Beghetto, 2006; Tierney & Farmer, 2002). Creative self-efficacy beliefs have been linked with students' motivational beliefs and academic aspirations (Beghetto, 2006), creativity ratings from supervisors (Tierney & Farmer, 2002), teachers' ratings of elementary students' creative expression (Beghetto, Kaufman, & Baxter, 2011), elementary students' subject matter learning (Beghetto & Baxter, 2012), and students' willingness to take intellectual risks in the classroom (Beghetto, 2009a).

The reason why efficacy beliefs are so important is that they help determine whether students will put forth the effort necessary for creative expression. Indeed, as Bandura (1997) has explained, "innovativeness requires an unshakeable sense of efficacy to persist in creative endeavors" (p. 239). In this way, efficacy beliefs serve as a key enhancer to creative accomplishment—providing the confidence and persistence necessary to move from mini-c creative ideation to larger-c creative expression and achievement.

Moreover, unless students have confidence in their ideas, it is very unlikely that they will be willing to take the risk necessary to share those ideas in the context of the classroom. Creative self-efficacy, therefore, can be thought of as a precursor to intellectual risk-taking. Intellectual risk-taking refers to "engaging in adaptive learning behaviors (sharing tentative ideas, asking questions, attempting to do and learn new things) that place the learner at risk of making mistakes or appearing less competent than others" (Beghetto, 2009a, p. 210).

Such behaviors are "risky" because they involve uncertainty (Byrnes, 1998) and carry perceived and real costs for students (e.g., being viewed as inferior in the eyes of one's peers and teachers). However, when students have a supportive environment and have confidence in their own ideas, they are more likely to see risks as challenging opportunities rather than threats. This is important because creativity involves taking risks. Indeed, as Sternberg (2010) has noted, nearly every invention and creative breakthrough involved some level of risk-taking.

Moreover, findings from prior research have linked intellectual risk-taking with student learning, academic identity development, and creative self-beliefs (Donovan & Bransford, 2005; Clifford, 1991; Clifford & Chou, 1991). When it comes to classroom learning, intellectual risk-taking and related self-beliefs often work together. In science, for instance, results from a recent study (Beghetto & Baxter, 2012) indicate that elementary students who had higher levels of creative self-efficacy were more willing to take intellectual risks when learning science and, in turn, were more likely to receive higher ratings of science understanding from their teachers.

Teachers can do much to support the development of their students' healthy self-beliefs by encouraging creative expression and providing informative feedback on students' creative potential and ability. Indeed, prior research has indicated that being told to be creative can result in higher levels of actual creative performance (Hennessey, 2010a; O'Hara & Sternberg, 2001). Encouraging creative expression and providing informative feedback also includes helping students develop an active self-awareness of their creative strengths and limitations (Beghetto & Kaufman, 2007). Such feedback helps ensure that students have a more accurate sense of their current level of creative competence and also how they might continue to develop their competence. This is particularly important given that prior research has found that students sometimes underestimate their creative ability (Beghetto, Kaufman, & Baxter, 2011) or feel that their teachers do not listen to them and have given up on them (Beghetto, 2006).

In sum, students' self-beliefs should not be viewed as an end-in-themselves, but rather as a creativity enhancer—increasing the likelihood that students will take the risks necessary to share, receive feedback on, and thereby develop their mini-c creative ideas into larger-c contributions. Teachers play a particularly important role in helping students calibrate and develop healthy self-beliefs by providing frequent and informative feedback. In the long run, the development of healthy self-beliefs can pay off in the form of helping students develop the stamina necessary to sustain effort, challenge themselves, and overcome the obstacles and setbacks that inhere in most any creative pursuit.

CONCLUDING THOUGHTS

The purpose of this chapter was to provide teachers with ideas for how to develop a creativity supportive classroom. Importantly, such efforts do not require adopting radically new curricula, instructional approaches, or activities. Rather teachers can establish a creativity supportive environment by developing an active understanding of how the motivational messages sent by their classroom activities and interactions can impact student motivation and creativity. This involves monitoring how students are experiencing the more tacit motivational messages being sent by the classroom learning tasks and assignments.

In addition to monitoring how students are experiencing everyday learning tasks and assignments, some of the most direct and potentially influential ways that teachers can support the development of students' self-beliefs are to incorporate students' interests in learning activities, support students' autonomy, help students develop healthy self-beliefs, and provide informative feedback to help students learn how to further develop their academic and creative competence.

Understanding how the school and classroom environment impact creativity sets the stage for more purposefully incorporating creativity into the everyday curriculum. Chapter 8 provides an overview of various strategies, insights, and examples of how teachers might build on the insights presented in this chapter.

CHAPTER 8

SMALL WINS

Incorporating Creativity into the Everyday Curriculum

By itself, one small win may seem unimportant...however...Once a small win has been accomplished, forces are set in motion that favor another small win ...[and the] next solvable problem often becomes more visible.
—Weick, 1984, p. 43

When it comes to incorporating creativity in the classroom, there are many ways that teachers can attempt to do so. Approaches can range on a continuum from making slight curricular adjustments (e.g., adding or reworking existing assignments and learning tasks) to making larger-scale additions (e.g., developing multi-week creativity projects). Curricular time and space, however, are finite. Adding more to the curriculum will at some point result in having to make decisions about what to cut. Given this important limitation, the most fruitful approaches seem to be located on the slight-change end of the continuum.

Killing Ideas Softly? The Promise and Perils of Creativity in the Classroom, pages 119–135.

This chapter will focus on how teachers might make slight adjustments to what they are already doing. In this way, teachers can discover ways to use creativity to complement (rather than compete with) their existing curriculum. As teachers become more aware of and comfortable with making one or two slight changes, then it is likely that additional opportunities will become more visible (just as Weick's opening quote asserts). Indeed, small curricular changes can accrue and make large differences in how students experience the classroom learning environment and, in turn, increase their willingness to express and develop their creative potential. In this way, when teachers make slight adjustments to what they are already doing, the cumulative creative outcome of those changes can be substantial.

Where might a teacher begin? One way to answer this question is to think about incorporating creativity in the classroom as occurring in three interrelated ways: teaching *about*, teaching *for*, and teaching *with* creativity. Each approach, including how teachers might incorporate these approaches into their curriculum, is discussed in the sections that follow.

TEACHING ABOUT CREATIVITY

When it comes to teaching *about* creativity, the teacher's goal is to help students learn about the nature of creativity so that they might be able to recognize the importance of creativity in their own learning and life. This includes how creativity is defined, what it looks like, common misconceptions, and how it develops (see Plucker & Dow, 2010). Teaching about creativity also includes helping students learn about findings from creativity research that have explored creative persons, processes, products, and contexts (Rhodes, 1961).

Examples of how teachers might teach *about* creativity in the regular curriculum include everything from providing students with subject area examples of accomplished creators (e.g., famous writers, mathematicians, scientists, historians), discussing the specific accomplishments of those creators, exploring the circumstances that supported and challenged those accomplishments, and learning about the process by which such accomplishments were recognized across history and how those accomplishments contributed to people and cultures across time (Beghetto & Kaufman, 2010a; Piirto, 2004). One of the best ways to do this is to include biographies of legendary creators in and across the teaching of regular academic subject matter areas.

Incorporating biographies of accomplished creators in the curriculum can help capture students' imagination and bring academic subject matter to life (Beghetto & Kaufman, 2010a). Moreover, including compelling life stories of key contributors to a field can spark important questions about creativity and academic subject matter such as: Who were the progenitors of the ideas and events we are studying about in math, science, history, and language arts? How were advances made in this field of study? Who gets to decide what counts as knowledge? What types of chance opportunities, access to resources, and supports allowed for these accomplishments? What kinds of setbacks did legendary creators face, and how did they overcome such setbacks? How many years of sustained effort are required for such contributions?

In addition to including biographies of legendary creators, teachers can also have students learn about the kinds of knowledge, strategies, and preparation necessary for professional levels of creative accomplishment in various academic fields (Beghetto & Kaufman, 2010a). One way to do this is to invite professionals (e.g., writers, engineers, artists, architects, and scientists) to visit the classroom (face-to-face or virtually through online video chat). Students can then engage these invited professionals in discussions that explore everything from the way the professionals first learned about the topics that the students are studying, the kinds of academic preparation that were necessary for them to go on to become professionals, how creativity has played a role in their everyday work, and how their creative accomplishments are shared with and assessed by others (e.g., peers, clients, and critics). Hearing from creative professionals can help spark and develop students' interest, provide a concrete example of the kind of creative work that is possible in various academic domains, and illustrate how creativity plays a role in and across various professions.

In addition to engaging professionals in discussions, teachers can also teach about creativity as part of developing a broader understanding of the nature of a particular academic subject area (Beghetto & Kaufman, 2010a). Math teachers, for instance, can help their students explore the role that the creative imagination plays in mathematical thinking and reasoning (e.g., the aesthetic aspects of visually representing quantitative data or how mathematicians visualize and work with highly abstract concepts). Language arts teachers can have their students consider how poets have used language and grammar in new and highly original ways or how reading various genres of literature can capture one's imagination. Science teachers can have their students learn the creative and imaginative ways that scientists approach their topics of investigation (e.g., how they find problems to explore, ways in which they inquire into scientific phenomena, and how approaches to scientific inquiry vary across different scientific disciplines).

Teaching *about* creativity also involves discussing creative thinking and problem-solving techniques with students and showing them how they are typically used to generate creative ideas and solutions. Teachers can also use these techniques as part of teaching regular academic subject areas. For instance, Professor Alexinia Baldwin (2010) provides an overview of several techniques that teachers might include in their everyday teaching. SCAMPER (Eberle, 1996) is an example. SCAMPER is a mnemonic that stands for substitute, combine, adapt, modify, put to another use, eliminate, and reverse. SCAMPER can be used in most any subject area to incorporate divergent thinking and generate creative outcomes. When teaching writing, for instance, teachers can have students read a story and *eliminate* a key scene or character and write how the story changes as a result. Math teachers might, for example, provide students with a number and have students work in *reverse* to demonstrate what different types of algebraic formulations could result in that number.

To summarize, the central goal of teaching *about* creativity is to introduce students to findings and insights from the field of creativity studies. This includes incorporating these insights into the teaching of academic subject matter. Moreover, when students become more aware of the nature of creativity and its relationship to academic subject areas, they will be in a better position to start using these insights in their own learning (e.g., using strategies like SCAMPER). In this way, teaching *about* creativity starts to blend with efforts aimed at teaching *for* creativity, which is the topic of the next section.

TEACHING FOR CREATIVITY

When proponents of creativity advocate for the inclusion of creativity in the classroom, they typically are referring to teaching *for* creativity. Teaching *for* creativity is aimed at developing students' creative potential into creative achievement. As has been discussed, creative achievements start with initial ideational sparks or mini-c insights of the creator (Beghetto & Kaufman, 2007b). This is true for the Big-C contributions of highly accomplished creators and the little-c classroom contributions of students. The difference between creators who are more accomplished and young students is that more accomplished creators have the awareness, confidence, experience, and subject matter expertise necessary for moving their personal mini-c insights into larger-c, recognizable creative contributions.

Although most students' mini-c insights will not lead to Big-C creative contributions, all students have the capacity to make contributions that are recognized as creative in (and perhaps beyond) the context of their classroom. In order for this to happen, however, students need support from their teachers so that they can develop the awareness and capacity to develop their mini-c insights into little-c contributions that are recognizable to others (Beghetto, 2007b). One way for teachers to do this is to provide opportunities for students to share, test-out, and refine their mini-c ideas. Doing so requires the combination of encouraging students to share their own ideas and providing clearly defined constraints—such as those offered by the conventions of the various academic subject areas. An example will help illustrate how this might be accomplished.

Teaching for Creativity in Math: An Example

Consider the example of a third grade math teacher in China who simultaneously teaches for creativity and mathematical learning (reported in Niu & Zhou, 2010). Professors Weihua Niu and Zheng Zhou explain that the teacher was able to accomplish both goals by simply making a slight adjustment to what many math teachers already do. Specifically, she not only asked students to share their work when solving problems (a typical approach), she also required that students approach math problems from multiple perspectives, using as many different methods to analyze and solve a problem as possible. Put simply, she actively encouraged her students to *come up with and share as many solutions as possible when solving problems.* This very simple, small adjustment establishes the conditions for students' creative ideation to flourish.

The following example, adapted from Niu and Zhou (2010, p. 277), is illustrative of this approach and provides a small sample of the variety of creative solutions that it can generate. Using the following problem, the teacher asked her students to come up with as many solutions as possible (directly encouraging students' creative ideation):

> The distance of a railway between the south and north sides of a city is 357 kilometers. An express train starts from the north; simultaneously, a local train starts from the south. The two trains run toward each other. In three hours, the two trains met. The speed of the express train is 79 kilometers per hour. How many kilometers less does the local train travel per hour than the express train on average?

Using this problem and encouraging students to present as many solutions as possible can result in a vast array of student solutions to this problem. Below are a few examples, adapted from the fifteen unique solutions presented in Niu and Zhou (2010, pp. 277–278).

> *Student 1:* $[357 - (79 \times 3)] / 3] = [357 - 237] / 3 = 120 / 3 = 40$ (km). The local train travels 40 km/hour. We already know that the express train travels 79 km/hour; therefore, $79 - 40 = 39$ (km). The local train travels 39 km less per hour on average than the express train.

> *Student 2:* $79 - (357 / 3 - 79) = 39$ (km).

> *Student 4:* Suppose the local train travels x km per hour, $(79 + x) \times 3 = 357$; $237 + 3x = 357$; $3x = 120$; $x = 40$; $79 - 40 = 39$ (km).

> *Student 9:* Suppose the local train travels x km less than the express train per hour, $(79 - x) \times 3 + 79 \times 3 = 357$; $474 - 3x = 357$; $3x = 117$; $x = 39$ (km).

As this example illustrates, requiring students to come up with and share as many solutions to the problem as possible allows the teacher to both promote mathematical thinking and support the development of creative competence. Specifically, by asking students to generate different solutions, the teacher was stimulating students' mini-c thinking (i.e., develop new insights for this problem based on their prior knowledge). Moreover, because students were encouraged to publicly share these various mini-c insights, students had the opportunity to contribute to the expansion and deepening of their own, their peers', and possibly even their teacher's mathematical and creative problem solving competence. In this way, the teacher was teaching *for* creativity by helping her students move from mini-c (internal) insights to little-c (public) contributions. This "both/and" approach—aimed at simultaneously developing academic and creative thinking—is at the core of teaching *for* creativity in the classroom. As Niu and Zhou (2010) note, "Solid foundation and skills in mathematics are indispensable to the development of mathematical creativity" (p. 279).

The "both/and" approach to teaching *for* creativity resolves the common "either/or" misconception that teaching academic skills and content knowledge requires the abandonment of creativity (Beghetto, 2010a) and, conversely, that focusing on creativity requires the abandonment of academic subject matter (Baer & Garrett, 2010). Indeed, creativity researchers from around the globe have documented how blending creativity in the curriculum can occur both in day-to-day teaching and in the assessment of domain-specific knowledge (cf., Beghetto & Kaufman, 2010a). One way to make sure this happens is to incorporate teaching *for* creativity in the planning of subject-matter-specific instructional activities and assessments.

Ideas for Incorporating Creativity in Lesson Planning

One reason why creativity is not included in everyday teaching of the classroom is that it is not included in the design and planning of lessons. Unless teachers plan for creativity, it becomes very difficult to cultivate students' creative competence in the structure of the taught lesson. As a result, creativity is planned out of the lesson. This is a form of creative suppression that results from what Professor Jeffery Smith has described as "the tyranny of the lesson plan" (personal communication, August 16, 2008). Fortunately, this can be avoided.

In order to teach for creativity, teachers need to allot some small portion of instructional time in their lesson plan for divergent thought and the exploration of unexpected student ideas. By planning for these moments of creative expression, teachers put themselves in a better position to recognize and develop students' creative potential. Moreover, doing so will signal to students that their mini-c ideas are important and, in turn, help cultivate the confidence and willingness necessary for students to share their mini-c conceptions.

In this way, teaching for creativity requires planning for creativity. One way for teachers to do this is to systematically build expectations for creative expression into their typical instructional planning routine. The following four steps serve as an example of how this can be done (adapted from Fairweather & Cramond, 2010, p. 124).

Steps for Lesson Planning

- *Step 1: Select a curricular goal or objective.* As with all lesson planning, this first step involves establishing an instructional goal or objective. The slight difference here is identifying broad enough goals and objectives that "leave room for exploration" and include opportunities for students to "analyze," "evaluate," "recognize," "distinguish," "explore," or "shape" academic content (Fairweather & Cramond, 2010).
- *Step 2: Identify thinking skills.* This step involves identifying what types of thinking skills students might use to obtain the learning goal or objective. Spending time identifying possible thinking skills sets the stage for recognizing and choosing a creative thinking skill that can be incorporated into the lesson. To assist with this process Fairweather and Cramond (2010) suggest that teachers attempt to answer such questions as: Do students need to generate various ideas about the topic covered in the lesson? Do students need to make connections between things to generate these ideas, or do they need to be flexible in their thinking and generate as many new ideas as possible?
- *Step 3: Select a creative thinking strategy.* Once the goals, objectives, and thinking skills have been identified, teachers are then ready to select a creative thinking strategy that will allow students to attain their goal and demonstrate their proficiency. Fairweather and Cramond (2010) highlight a variety of creative strategies that can be used, including viewing issues from multiple perspectives, making analogies, and using techniques like SCAMPER. Becoming familiar with idea generation strategies and idea evaluation strategies will allow teachers to see new connections between their academic goals and how creative thinking strategies can be used to attain those goals.
- *Step 4: Design instructional activities.* Finally, once teachers have identified their academic goals, thinking skills, and creative thinking strategies that can be used to attain those goals, they are then ready to design, or better yet, modify existing activities so as to simultaneously teach for creativity and academic learning. A science teacher might, for example, modify an existing science project lesson using SCAMPER (Eberle, 1996). Rather than focus on one field of study for a project (e.g., chemistry or biology), the teacher could require students to *combine* two fields, like technology and health, to identify a

question that could be explored scientifically (e.g., How might social media technology be used to help promote healthy eating habits?).

The steps above are similar to guidelines aimed at teaching for creativity that have been developed in the United Kingdom. Professor Anna Craft (2010), for instance, reports how teachers have been encouraged to adopt a pedagogical approach that endeavors to simultaneously support creativity and learning. This includes establishing clear criteria for success, capitalizing on the unexpected without losing sight of the original academic learning objectives, asking open-ended questions, encouraging openness to ideas and critical reflection, and regularly reviewing students' work in progress.

When teachers have the simultaneous goals of teaching for creativity and academic learning, they need to strike a balance between providing corrective feedback on students' understanding of academic subject matter and, at the same time, encouraging students to share their mini-c ideas (Beghetto & Kaufman, 2007). One way for teachers to encourage students to share and refine their mini-c ideas is to ask exploratory questions (such as "I wasn't expecting that…can you help us understand how that idea fits with our discussion?" or "Can you provide an example of what you mean?"). Then, after having explored such ideas, teachers need to provide students with evaluative feedback to help them learn when and why their ideas do (and do not) seem to fit the particular situation (Beghetto, 2007b).

The above approach can be summarized in the following simple reminder: *Explore first. Then evaluate.* Developing the habit of exploring first and then evaluating can help teachers avoid the temptation of immediately evaluating the correctness of students' ideas and, instead, approach students' unique ideas and interpretations with a sense of curiosity and willingness to understand the potential fit of those ideas. Sometimes this will lead to development of students' mini-c ideas into meaningful little-c contributions; other times this will lead to helping students revise or abandon their ideas in search of more accurate or task appropriate conceptions (Beghetto, 2007b).

In sum, a large part of teaching for creativity requires planning for creativity. This, in turn, requires developing a habit of exploring students' unexpected contributions and then working with students to evaluate the appropriateness and fit of those contributions. In this way, teaching for creativity also requires assessing for creativity.

Ideas for Incorporating Creativity into Assessments

Including creativity as part of classroom assessments is, arguably, one of the most important things teachers can do to encourage student creativity. This is because assessments, more so than many other feature of the learning environment, signal to students what is *really* important (Beghetto, 2010a). Put another way, what you assess is what you get when it comes to classroom learning. Unless teachers include creativity in their classroom assessments, students likely won't take the risk of being creative and instead simply reproduce what the teacher expects to see or hear.

Recall from Chapter 5 Guilford's (1950) anecdote about the college professor who assigned a paper to his students and informed them that they would be graded on originality. One student, however, knew that even though the professor asked for originality, what he really valued were his own pet ideas. The student therefore simply strung together the professor's transcribed lecture notes and ideas. She in turn received an "A" on the paper. And her professor informed her that the paper was one of the most original papers he had ever read.

Guilford's anecdote illustrates that assessments serve as one of the clearest signals of what is valued in the classroom. This is why, regardless of what teachers might otherwise say about how interesting or important something is, students often will ask, "Yes, but will it be on the test?" It is therefore important that teachers include and evaluate creativity in their assignments and assessments. But how might they go about doing so? Should teachers select a pre-existing measure and try to incorporate it into their existing assessments?

There are many existing creativity assessments that educators can use (and have used) to assess student creativity in schools and classrooms (see Kaufman, Plucker, & Baer, 2008; Plucker & Makel, 2010 for a review). Such measures, however, typically are used to make placement decisions in gifted and talented programs or to conduct classroom-based creativity research. As such, teachers also need ways to assess creativity that can be easily incorporated into the learning assessments they already use in their classroom. Fortunately, creativity researchers have started to develop subject matter assessments that can be integrated into teachers' existing classroom assessments.

One example is a reading comprehension task developed by Professor Elena Grigorenko and her colleagues (Grigorenko, Jarvin, Tan, & Sternberg, 2008), which assesses both academic and creative proficiency. With respect to assessing academic proficiency, Grigorenko and her team developed differing levels of reading comprehension. Whereas the lowest level of comprehension is represented by students being able to understand a central idea of a paragraph or locate a single bit of information in a passage, the highest level is represented by students being able to analyze the text, make inferences, draw conclusions, and justify their conclusions. With respect to creativity, the lowest level of proficiency is represented in students making slight modifications to details or ideas presented in the text, whereas the highest level of proficiency involves going beyond what was read by coming up with novel character developments, plot lines, and situations (Grigorenko et al. 2008).

As Grigorenko and her colleagues (2008) have explained, once these scales have been developed, they can be broken down into teachable exercises and activities that teachers can use to nurture student creativity and academic learning. As a result, teachers are able to incorporate and assess student creativity in and across most any subject area. Although the proficiency scales developed by Grigorenko and her team represent the efforts of measurement experts, classroom teachers can still draw inspiration from these efforts and use the overarching ideas of this approach as a guide for modifying their existing classroom assessments. Indeed, teachers who already use assessments to go beyond determining whether students can simply memorize and recall facts are already well on their way to incorporating creativity in their assessments.

All that these teachers need to do is make a few additional adjustments. Specifically, teachers need to make explicit the expectation that, in addition to being required to accurately represent their understanding of subject matter, students are also required to provide their own unique examples, uses, and applications of that subject matter. This also involves mapping out different levels of academic and creative proficiency.

One way to do this is to create a two-part rubric that can be used to assess both academic and creative proficiency. The following steps can serve as a starting point for helping teachers incorporate creativity into their existing assessments. These steps are adapted from steps for creating scoring rubrics (described in Mertler, 2001) and inspired by the work of Grigorenko and her colleagues (2008). Exhibit 8.1 is an example of how an initial draft of this kind of rubric might look.

Steps for Developing a Two-part Rubric

- *Step 1: Identify the academic process or product to be assessed.* When attempting to assess both academic learning and creativity, it is often helpful to identify the overall process (e.g., solving a math story problem), product (e.g., a science fair project), or performance (e.g., acting out key features of a historical event) that the teacher intends to assess. This holistic approach to assessments focuses more on overall quality, proficiency, and demonstration of skills and is particularly desirable when the learning activity or task requires students to provide a creative response (Mertler, 2001)—that is, a response that allows for multiple ways to approach the process, solution, outcomes, or resulting products. Taking a more holistic approach to assessment

EXHIBIT 8.1.   Mathematical Problem Solving—Example Rubric

Academic		Creative	
Level of proficiency	Description	Level of proficiency	Description
4 Aspirational	Able to solve highly complex problems using more advanced or specialized mathematical knowledge.	4 Aspirational	Student solves a particularly complex problem using novel methods that might be used by professional mathematicians.
3 Accomplished	Uses appropriate methods. Makes no mistakes. Sound explanations of thinking.	3 Accomplished	The student approaches a problem from a highly unique—yet task appropriate—perspective (e.g., "Sean's numbers" in Chapter 3).
2 Developing	Uses appropriate methods. Makes few mistakes. Offers explanations of thinking.	2 Developing	The student uses a novel and accurate approach to solving the problem (e.g., Gary's reasoning in Chapter 3).
1 Emerging	Uses an inappropriate approach. Makes mistakes. Offers no explanation of thinking.	1 Emerging	The student tries using a previously modeled method or combination of methods that is new to him or her (but not new to others); Or Uses a novel, but mathematically inaccurate approach.
0 No Attempt	No response or attempt	0 No attempt	Task not attempted
Academic Proficiency Score	—	Creative Proficiency Score	—

Note. Academic and creative proficiency descriptions inspired by Mertler (2012) and Grigorenko et al. (2008).

lends itself well to making a connection between academic learning and creative expression.

- *Step 2: Identify indicators of academic proficiency.* Once the academic process, product, or performance has been determined, the next step is to develop the academic portion of the rubric by identifying observable indicators of academic proficiency. Observable indicators refer to the skills, behaviors, concepts, and types of understanding that teachers would like their students to demonstrate in the academic process, product, or performance (Mertler, 2001). Key questions to address during this stage include: What does it look like when students have not yet developed their proficiency (for this particular academic process, product, or performance)? What does it look like when students are starting to develop their proficiency? What does it look like once students are proficient (and where might they go from here)?

- *Step 3: Develop descriptions of academic proficiency.* Once different levels of proficiency have been identified, teachers can then develop descriptions of each performance level along the continuum from the lowest (emerging level) to the highest (most accomplished level) of proficiency (Mertler, 2001). The highest levels of proficiency can also include aspirational levels of proficiency that go well beyond the reach of most students. This can help students understand what expert performance might look like in a particular subject area and what additional learning is needed to arrive at this level of performance. Of course, teachers need to use their discretion when including these expert levels of performance to make sure that they are viewed as aspirational, rather than demoralizing. Once each level has been delineated, teachers need to include examples of each proficiency level. One of the best ways to do so is to include actual samples of student work that represent each of the levels. Initially, sample work may not be available. As such, teachers will need to rely on vivid descriptions. The more descriptive and illustrative each of these levels is, the more likely students will be to understand them and the easier it will be for teachers and students to identify students' current level of proficiency.

- *Step 4: Identify indicators of creative expression.* Similar to identifying indicators of academic proficiency, developing the creative portion of the rubric involves identifying differing levels of creative expression. Teachers can find guidance for doing so from models of creative performance such as the Propulsion Theory of Creativity (Sternberg, Kaufman, & Pretz, 2002) introduced in Chapter 1. Recall that the theory outlines eight different types of creative contributions, ranging from those types that accept and work within a particular domain to contributions that attempt to redefine and transform a domain. Teachers can draw on these different types of creative contribution to develop classroom-appropriate indicators of differing levels of creative expression. Key questions to address during this stage include: What does it look like when the students are demonstrating the lowest level of creative proficiency—*replicating* some previously modeled or existing process, product, or performance? What does it look like when students are starting to develop their creative proficiency—*redefining* some previously modeled or existing process, product, or performance? What does it look like once students are proficient—*forward incrementing* or *redirecting* some previously modeled or existing process, product, or performance (and where might they go from here)?

- *Step 5: Develop descriptions and examples for each level of creative proficiency.* This step focuses on developing descriptions and providing examples (e.g., samples of previous students' work) highlighting the key attributes of the performance, product, or processes for each level of creative proficiency. Again, the more descriptive and illustrative each of these levels is, the easier it will be for teachers and students to identify current and more advanced levels of creative proficiency. Including aspirational levels of creative proficiency can also help students recognize what more expert or highly accomplished levels of creative proficiency look like in this particular academic domain.

- *Step 6: Test-out, revise, and refine.* Rubric development and refinement is an ongoing, iterative process. As such, it requires constant testing, revision, and refinement to help ensure that the rubric is providing a consistent (i.e., reliable) and useful method of assessing the development of students' academic and creative proficiency. One way teachers can test out their rubrics is to have students, colleagues, and even parents use the rubrics to assess samples of student work and then discuss whether they are able to establish consistent scores. Ideally, a rubric can be used by most anyone to consistently assess differing levels of performance. Consistency in ratings is only one component of refining rubrics; the other is to invite colleagues, students, and (to the extent possible) subject matter experts to provide feedback on how the different levels of proficiency are being described and represented in the rubric. In addition to getting feedback on the rubrics, monitoring how well performance on the rubric aligns with other indicators of learning and creative performance is another way for teachers to assess the usefulness of the rubric. Finally, teachers can collect samples of student work, which can be used as examples for subsequent students. Doing so can go a long way in helpings students understand differing levels of proficiency and how they might improve upon their current levels of proficiency.

The math problem-solving rubric depicted in Exhibit 8.1 is meant to illustrate how a rubric might be developed that can be used to simultaneously assess academic and creative proficiency. Importantly, this scoring guide allows for various combinations of scores. For example, a student might attain an accomplished level of academic proficiency but still be at the emerging level in creative proficiency. In such cases, teachers can help the student develop his or her creative competence by providing opportunities for the student to come up with his or her own unique, yet still accurate, approach to solving math problems. With practice, teachers can find multiple opportunities to incorporate creativity into their teaching and assessment of academic learning.

Once teachers become familiar with and try out a few of these planning and assessment examples, it will become much easier for them to find ways to teach *for* creativity. Moreover, they will start to recognize additional ways to incorporate creativity in their classrooms by making slight adjustments to their existing lessons, learning activities, and assessments. Teachers may be surprised at just how easy it is to make such adjustments to their teaching and can judge for themselves whether such adjustments are having a meaningful impact on students' learning and creative development. When teachers consciously focus on ways to teach *for* creativity, they make the conditions more favorable for teaching *with* creativity.

TEACHING WITH CREATIVITY

Teaching *with* creativity is inextricably connected to teaching *for* creativity (Jeffrey & Craft, 2004). Indeed, when teachers are willing to approach teaching creatively, they establish a context that is conducive to catalyzing students' own creativity. This is because, as Lilly and Bramwell-Rejskind (2004) have asserted, creative teaching "provides a safe climate where students can [take intellectual risks] and push boundaries" (p. 104). A creativity safe environment starts with teachers espousing a value for creativity and demonstrating their appreciation of creativity by way of modeling a creative approach to teaching. This includes teachers demonstrating a willingness to take risks (such as trying to learn or do something new); learn from (rather than avoid) mistakes; accept uncertainty; seek out complexity; approach teaching and learning with flexible thinking and open-mindedness; seek out and explore diverse ideas, perspectives, and experiences; and demonstrate a deep commitment to and enjoyment of one's own learning process (Jeffrey & Craft, 2004; Lilly & Bramwell-Rejskind, 2004).

Teaching creatively, then, is really about approaching teaching as a creative act. In this way, creative teaching represents a form of improvisational performance. As mentioned in Chapter 2, the metaphor of "disciplined improvisation" (Sawyer, 2004) represents what is at the heart of creative teaching. This metaphor refers to teaching as a special form of improvisation that occurs within the broad structures and routines of the classroom. James Kaufman and I have elaborated on this metaphor (see Beghetto & Kaufman, 2011) and have described how teachers might use it to guide them as they teach for and with creativity. Specifically, we describe the disciplined part of the definition as referring to the fixed aspects of teaching (e.g., the academic subject matter that teachers are required to teach) and the improvisational part of the definition as referring to the fluid aspects of teaching (e.g., how teachers might approach their teaching of subject matter in various ways).

Creative teaching therefore involves combining structure and flexibility in both the planning and actual moment-to-moment teaching of a lesson. The simple "fixed or fluid" heuristic can serve as a reminder for teachers to actively consider what aspects of their lessons might need to be more fixed (e.g., the required elements of writing up a report of a science experiment) and what aspects can be more fluid (e.g., students selecting their own topic of scientific inquiry). This active consideration of the fluid and fixed heuristic occurs both during teachers' planning of lessons and during the moment-to-moment decision making of teaching. Indeed, as Jeffrey and Craft (2004) have explained, opportunities to teach creatively and teach for creativity can (and often do) "arise spontaneously from teaching situations in which it was not specifically intended" (p. 14).

Being mindful of this "fixed or fluid" heuristic can help teachers confidently engage micromoment opportunities (see Chapter 2), recognizing that they need not hold desperately to the planned curriculum but rather take ownership of the moment and determine whether it might be beneficial to make an initially "fixed" aspect of the planned curriculum more "fluid." When teachers do so, they can realize the creative potential that inheres in such opportunities. One way to think about this is to recognize that approaching teaching creatively is akin to approaching life creatively. Both require engaging one's imagination, seeking out new experiences, exploring the unknown with curiosity (instead of fear), considering multiple possibilities, taking sensible risks, and learning (often in unexpected ways) from our experiences. What might this look like during an actual lesson?

Moving Between the Fluid and Fixed: Classroom Examples

A few quick examples can help illustrate how teachers can (and sometimes need to) move between fluid and fixed aspects of teaching. The first example is adapted from a fifth grade math lesson (reported in Lampert, 1990). The teacher has planned a lesson with the goal of helping her students develop their understanding of exponents. Specifically, the teacher planned some introductory activities and has students work through several examples to help them develop their understanding. At one point in the lesson, one student (Sam) asserts that the last digit in the solution to 5^4 "has to end in 5" (p. 48).

At this point, the teacher is confronted with a decision: does she allow the planned lesson to become more fluid and invite all students to test the viability of this assertion, or does she step-in, provide a quick explanation, and move the students along to the next planned problem of the lesson? The teacher chose the former, inviting her students to engage Sam's assertion, asking the class: "How does he know that is true?" (p. 48). By doing so the teacher created a fluid opportunity for her students to share and test out their own unique and personally meaningful (mini-c) conceptions.

More specifically, the teacher provided her students with the fluidity necessary for them to initiate and engage in an unplanned and content-rich exploration of mathematical reasoning. The students were able to test out and eventually justify their ideas and thereby move from initial mini-c interpretations into little-c contributions. Because the teacher was willing to explore the fluid, unplanned moment, she was able to realize the creative learning potential of this curricular micromoment. Doing so went well beyond the initially planned problems and resulted in rather sophisticated learning about the nature of mathematics itself.

This is nicely illustrated in one excerpt from a student (Carl) who presents an explanation that moves beyond a particular problem and serves as a mathematical generalization, which as Lampert (1990) explains, directs "the class's attention to what doing mathematics means" (p. 49). Specifically, Carl asserted, "You don't have to do that [figure out that 5^4 is 625]. Its easy, the *last digit is always going to be 5* because you are always multiplying last digits of 5, and 5 times 5 ends in a 5" (p. 49).

As illustrated in this example, when teachers are willing to change the fixed lesson into fluid moments of student-initiated exploration, they create new opportunities for creative expression and deeper subject matter learning. Of course, there are also times when teachers need to make in-the-moment decisions about whether initially "fluid" aspects might benefit from becoming more "fixed" so as to avoid student confusion and potential curricular chaos.

Consider this next example of a middle school math teacher (Ann), reported in Nathan and Knuth (2003). As a result of her participation in a research project, Ann established a goal of wanting to involve her students more in classroom interactions. Her early efforts in doing so, unfortunately, resulted in losing sight of when it was also necessary to make a lesson more fixed and teacher-directed.

Consequently, as Nathan and Knuth (2003) explained, student confusion and competing conceptions of mathematical concepts went unresolved. When students needed help constructing or verifying correct mathematical ideas, their teacher was not "participating as a mathematical authority" (p. 197). An example of this is illustrated in the following excerpt from one of Ann's lessons in which students were trying to understand factors:

Brad: [A factor is] a number multiplied by another number to get the
   answer.
Darias: A number that goes evenly into another number.
Kenny: I think it's for multiplication and subtraction.
Bob: I think it's for multiplication. No, I think it's for everything.
Anthony: Let's vote!

As the above excerpt illustrates, if teachers do not know when to intervene during the flow of student ideas, they can contribute to subject matter confusion. Moreover, as has been discussed throughout this book, teaching creatively requires providing adequate subject matter support and constraints. Consequently, if students frequently face situations where they are asked to engage with academic subject matter but are not provided with the resources, teacher support, or capacity to arrive at accurate understanding, they likely will mistrust their own conceptions or their teacher's invitations to share their conceptions. As such, it is imperative that teachers know when to step in and support students to help resolve student confusion and uncertainty. Otherwise, something as arbitrary as voting on definitions can seem "as reasonable as any other method for establishing the definitions of [subject-matter] terms" (Nathan & Knuth, 2003, p. 198).

Taken together, thoughtful planning and the ability to move between the fixed and fluid aspects of teaching represent a core characteristic of teaching creatively. Indeed, creative teaching requires an approach to lesson preparation and actual instruction that involves cycling between thoughtful consideration of the more fluid and fixed aspects when planning lessons and spontaneous, instructional decision-making when teaching.

CONCLUDING THOUGHTS

Incorporating creativity in the classroom does not require adopting radically new curricula, instructional approaches, activities, or assessments. Rather, teachers can support student creativity by making slight, incremental changes to what they already do in the classroom. These slight changes require teachers to approach their planning, in-the-moment teaching, and assessments with creativity in mind.

With practice, teachers can move toward developing a nearly seamless instructional approach that blends creativity with academic learning. This requires that teachers view themselves as creative and approach the act of teaching (and life itself) with a spirit of possibility, openness, imagination, and creativity.

Unless we, as educators, are willing to approach our own teaching, learning, and life with creativity, it is unlikely that we will be able to communicate or model the importance of doing so for our students. Indeed, no set of creative strategies, creative activities, or creative curricula can replace the value of trying to approach one's teaching with a creativity supportive stance. Sometimes this requires providing ourselves with simple reminders. The final chapter provides fifteen reminders aimed at helping teachers develop and maintain a creative mindset.

CHAPTER 9

CARRYING CREATIVITY FOREWORD

A Distillation of Instructional Reminders and Resources

The classroom with all its limitations remains a location of possibility.
—hooks, 1994, p. 207

As the opening quote asserts, the classroom, even with all its limitations, is a site of possibility—a place where students and teachers can engage in possibility thinking (Craft, 2005) and move from *what is* to *what could* or *should be* (Greene, 1995). The previous chapters in this book had the goal of helping teachers develop an applied understanding of creativity in the classroom—highlighting both opportunities and potential pitfalls. The chapters also had the goal of sparking teachers' own ideas for how they might approach their teaching with a creativity-supportive stance.

The purpose of this final chapter is twofold. First, I provide a summary of 15 instructional reminders that can serve as quick touchstones and summaries of key themes addressed throughout the book. I encourage readers to return to these 15 reminders often—reflecting on them, discussing them with colleagues, and adding them to ongoing efforts to meaningfully incorporate creativity into their everyday curriculum.

The second purpose of this chapter is to point to additional resources where readers can find more information about creativity and its relationship to teaching and learning. To this end, I have highlighted various sources that can keep teachers up-to-date with respect to new advances and insights in the field of creativity studies.

FIFTEEN INSTRUCTIONAL REMINDERS

1. *Creativity is more than originality.* One of the most important things teachers can do to help ensure that creativity has a place in their classrooms is to help deepen students' and their own understanding of the nature of creativity itself. As was discussed in Chapter 1, creativity requires more than originality. It also requires that an original contribution makes sense for a given situation, context, or problem. There are also different types and levels of creativity—ranging from slight innovations (modifying an existing story) and mini-c personal insights (a child coming up with a new and personally meaningful metaphor for a scientific concept) to radically new transformations (the *iPhone*) and legendary Big-C creators and contributions (John Coltrane's revolutionary jazz style). Finally, although we all have creative potential, developing that potential into creative achievement requires hard work, sustained effort, and the development of one's domain-specific knowledge.

2. *Creativity and academic learning are complementary.* A common roadblock for teachers who want to incorporate creativity in their classrooms is to mistakenly believe that creativity and learning are in competition with each other. This, in large part, is due to how creativity and learning have historically been conceptualized. If learning is viewed as the reproduction of existing knowledge and creativity is viewed as original thought, then it would make sense that trying to cultivate learning and creativity would be an either/ or decision: "Either I spend time having students memorize and reproduce what they memorized" or "I spend time helping students develop their ability to come up with new ideas." If teachers come to believe these common views about learning and creativity, then creativity will almost always come out on the losing end of the equation (see Chapters 4 and 5). Fortunately, this need not be the case. As was discussed in Chapter 3, decades of work in the learning sciences and creativity studies has demonstrated how creativity

and learning are complementary processes. This is good news for teachers because it helps them engage in the possibility thinking necessary for incorporating creativity into their lesson planning, teaching, and assessments (see Chapter 8). When teachers recognize this connection, they can approach nurturing creativity and subject matter teaching with a both/and (rather than either/or) perspective.

3. *You have to learn to think inside the box before you can think outside of it.* "Thinking outside the box" is, arguably, the most commonly associated description of creative thinking. The problem with this phrase is that it can imply that creativity requires elimination of all constraints. As was discussed in Chapter 1, creativity always involves constraints (Sternberg & Kaufman, 2010). This is because there are no constraint-free environments (constraints always impinge upon us), and, more importantly, constraints provide the parameters necessary for determining whether something is creative (rather than simply original). In the context of the classroom, those constraints include academic subject matter conventions, assignment guidelines, and the various other learning requirements specified for a given learning activity, assignment, or task. Helping students understand that creativity is best thought of as a form of "constrained originality" (Keller & Keller, 1996) can go a long way in supporting students' creative potential. Specifically, teachers can help students recognize that if they attempt to be creative without adhering to constraints, then their efforts will more likely result in frustration and confusion, rather than a meaningful creative contribution. Indeed, as I have noted elsewhere (Beghetto, 2007b), "one has to be familiar with what it means to be 'inside the box' (i.e., aware of the conventions and standards of a domain or discipline) in order to think outside of it" (p. 266). Equipped with this understanding, teachers and students can focus their efforts on clarifying the nature of the task, what knowledge is necessary, and how students might put their own unique spin on classroom assignments, tasks, and activities (see also Chapter 8).

4. *Accomplished creators know when (and when not) to be creative.* With the increased emphasis placed on the importance of incorporating creativity in the classroom, teachers may get the message that it is necessary for them and their students to try to be creative at all times and in all contexts. Such an aspiration is both unattainable and unnecessary (Kaufman & Beghetto, in press). Rather than attempt to find ways to always make a creative contribution, teachers and students would do well to actively consider when and in what context creativity is worth the time, effort, and risk. Accomplished

creators learn to self-regulate when and how they express their creativity. This is because accomplished creators recognize that their contributions come with a cost. Creative contributions place the creator at risk of being rejected or misunderstood and can result in some degree of disruption in the experiences and environmental context that are shared by others. In the classroom, teachers can help students recognize when it might not be appropriate to try to make an original contribution given the constraints of a particular activity or task (e.g., writing a sonnet about algebra on a math exam). Teaching students when and how to be creative is not the same as discouraging creativity. Rather it is about helping students develop their self, contextual, and subject-matter knowledge (Kaufman & Beghetto, in press) so that they have the awareness, confidence, and willingness to make meaningful, creative contributions. Teachers can support this development by including biographies of accomplished creators (illustrating both their struggles and successes with creative expression) and by providing informative and supportive feedback to students as they express their own mini-c contributions (see Chapter 8).

5. *Creativity can't die, but it can be stifled.* Given recent concerns raised in the popular media about a "creativity crisis" (Bronson & Merryman, 2010), parents and teachers may worry that children's creativity is in grave danger. Although creativity can be suppressed in school and classroom settings, it really can't die. This is important for all advocates of creativity to understand as it can stave off the temptation to demonize schools for having caused irreversible damage to student creativity. As has been discussed, the stifling nature of schools and classrooms is not an *inherent* feature of schooling, but the result of some combination of inherited instructional practices, assumptions about creativity and learning, and pressures from external accountability mandates. Although these features can suppress creativity, creativity can always bounce back. Moreover, teachers can minimize the chances that creativity will be suppressed by being aware of factors that impede creative expression (see Chapters 4 & 5) and by monitoring how students are experiencing their classroom environment (see Chapter 7). In this way, teachers can take an active role in disrupting practices that have a basis in overly narrow conceptions of learning and, instead, adopt a more expansive view that allows for the simultaneous development of meaningful subject matter learning and creative expression (see Chapters 3 & 8). Indeed, the best way to prevent creative suppression is to actively encourage creative expression.

6. *Be aware of the potential for creative mortification.* Although creativity can't die, students' willingness to share and develop their creativity can be indefinitely suspended. Creative mortification is the indefinite suspension of creative expression following negative evaluative performance feedback. Specifically, when students share and seek feedback on their creative expression and experience negative feedback as evidence of a fixed, limited ability, then they are at more risk for feeling shamed by that experience and, as a result, experience creative mortification (see Chapter 6). As such, all educators—be they parents, teachers, or coaches—should be mindful of the type of feedback they provide to students and how that feedback is experienced by students (see also Chapter 7). This is not to say that educators should avoid negative evaluative feedback. Indeed, honest feedback is necessary for the growth and development of creative competence. Rather, what educators need to be mindful of is how that feedback is delivered and received. Specifically, all feedback—and particularly negative performance feedback—needs to be accompanied by information that zeroes in on what specifically needs improvement, provides some direction on next steps aimed at improving, and reinforces the idea that improvement is possible with continued effort. Of course there are no guarantees that such efforts will lead to highly accomplished levels of creativity, but at the very least, students can have a direction to take. This, in turn, will help ensure that students can continue to enjoy and develop their life-wide competence in that particular area of creative expression.

7. *Accomplished creators turn mini-c insights into creative contributions.* Accomplished creators have the experience, knowledge, and skill necessary to take their mini-c insights and develop them into creative contributions. Although it would take children many years of deliberate practice to become accomplished creators (Ericsson, 1996), teachers can still help students learn how to develop their creative potential into creative contributions. Indeed, one of the most important things teachers can do to support the development of students' creative competence is to help them learn how to grow their mini-c potential into little-c contributions. Specifically, teachers can encourage students to share their mini-c ideas, provide the kind of feedback necessary to develop and refine their ideas, and help students recognize when it might be appropriate to abandon ideas in favor of more viable ideas (Beghetto, 2007b; Chapters 2 & 3). Helping students learn how to develop their mini-c conceptions into creative contributions also involves helping students understand that creative ideas are often misunderstood and even

resisted. Indeed, as Sternberg (2010) has noted, creative ideas do not sell themselves. As such, teachers should provide students with opportunities to practice communicating the value of their ideas to other people. With practice and support from their teachers, students will gain confidence in their ability to convert their mini-c insights into little-c contributions.

8. *Try to see beyond the how to the what.* When students share their mini-c ideas and interpretations, they often do so in a way that is not very polished. Consequently, *what* is being communicated (i.e., the underlying creative potential or contribution) can get lost in *how* it is communicated (i.e., the unusual, unexpected delivery). In the rapid give-and-take of classroom discussions and activities, it is sometimes easy for teachers to dismiss and redirect potentially creative ideas (see Chapter 5). However, teachers can uncover meaningful creative contributions if they are willing to explore unexpected ideas (Chapter 2). The challenge that teachers face in such moments is that it is difficult to determine whether a surprising or unexpected student expression has its basis in misunderstanding, creative ideation, or even a willful attempt at disruption. Sometimes the only way a teacher can recognize the potential of a surprising student idea is to take a moment to look beyond the unusualness of *how* something is being presented or expressed to the *what* that lies beneath. One of the best and most direct ways a teacher can do so is to simply let the student know that the connection between the student's ideas and the task at hand is unclear, by saying something as simple as, "Can you help us understand how what you are saying fits with what we've been talking about?" Once teachers have a better understanding of how students have made the connection, they can then work with students to help develop the way they communicate their ideas—including helping students learn how to articulate their ideas within the expectations and constraints of particular assignments; providing more time for the student to "revise and resubmit" the idea or assignment; and even helping students recognize that an idea, insight, or expression doesn't fit the particular situation. Doing so can ensure that teachers recognize and develop students' creative potential.

9. *Monitor mini-motivational messages of the classroom.* Some of the most subtle, yet potentially powerful influences on creativity are the mini-motivational messages sent by the everyday routines, behaviors, and interactions of the classroom environment (Chapter 7). I call these mini-messages because they are often so subtle (and unintentional) that many teachers are unaware that these motivational messages are being communicated to students. The "mini"

label, however, should not be interpreted to mean that the impact is slight and not worth monitoring, but rather should signal to teachers that the small things in a classroom—everything from how students' work is recognized and rewarded to how informal feedback is delivered—warrant active attention. One way to think about mini-messages is to recognize that it is not so much about what is being communicated by any particular routine, procedure, or activity but rather how students experience those messages. Specifically, teachers should be careful that the mini-messages of the classroom being sent do not create an environment that can undermine students' creative motivation (Chapter 7; Hennessey, 2010a). Creativity supportive environments tend to send the following messages to students: You have time to think and work on tasks without needing to worry about constant surveillance from your teachers or peers; the primary goal in this classroom is self-improvement and how you are doing now in comparison to how you have done before; you have freedom to generate messy ideas, take intellectual risks, and try new things that might result in mistakes; and the reason why you put forth effort is that you see the value in the task, you are focused on improvement, and you are interested in and enjoy the task.

10. *Approach teaching with the eye of Monet.* When teachers approach surprising curricular moments with an eye of Monet, they view such moments as creative opportunities (Chapter 2). Doing so is easier said than done. One reason is that teaching is a goal directed activity, and it is therefore easy to be focused more on what will (or should) happen next as opposed to what is occurring in the present moment. When this happens it is easy to miss unplanned curricular opportunities or view them as signs of impending curricular chaos. Teachers who approach their teaching with an eye of Monet have developed the experience and in-the-moment mindfulness to recognize that unexpected turns in the curriculum are moments of creative potential that warrant exploration. Teachers who approach teaching with the eye of Monet have the experience to know that pursuing such opportunities carries risk—risk of losing precious curricular time, risk of following an unexpected student idea down a curricular rabbit-hole, risk of entering a curricular space that can lead to more confusion than insight. These teachers, therefore, also have the confidence and subject matter expertise necessary to recognize and appropriately respond to these curricular risks and opportunities.

11. *Hold your lesson plans lightly.* Teaching is a highly planned activity. Indeed, one of the first things prospective teachers learn is how

to plan a lesson. Implicit in this process is the idea (or hope) that chaotic classroom moments can be planned away by highly structured lessons. The good news is, creativity can and does thrive in structure. Structure provides the necessary constraints to serve as a counterbalance to originality (Chapter 1). Teaching for and with creativity (Chapter 8), however, requires arriving at a middle ground. This is because, in the context of the classroom, creativity is most likely found in the space between chaos and conformity: a flexibly structured middle ground. Experienced teachers know (and new teachers quickly come to realize) that no matter how much planning goes into a lesson, there will always be surprising moments. Indeed, the curriculum-as-planned never quite aligns with the curriculum-as-lived (Aoki, 2004; Chapter 2). Rather than attempt to "plan-away" or quickly dismiss unexpected moments, creative teachers prepare for them to occur and practice dwelling in those moments in an effort to evaluate whether such moments might lead to new and creative opportunities for student learning and the development of students' potential. As such, creative teachers approach unexpected moments with a sense of curiosity and willingness to explore those moments. Creative teachers also make in-the-moment decisions as to whether they need to be flexible with what they initially planned or whether it is necessary to return to the lesson as planned (Chapter 8). This in-the-moment awareness and responsiveness speaks to the art or even the dance of teaching—having the pedagogical intuition of knowing when to step away from the planned lesson and toward the unexpected opportunities and also knowing when to return to the lesson-as-planned. This sort of pedagogical expertise comes from practice, reflection, and, most importantly, the willingness to approach curricular uncertainty with confidence and curiosity (Chapter 8).

12. *Establish routines that ensure that ideas will be revisited.* Although it is important for teachers to take time to explore unexpected ideas (Chapters 3 & 5), it is not always possible to do so. In some cases, exploring an idea may require more time than a teacher has to offer. In other cases, a teacher may need to maintain a current direction so as to avoid confusion. In short there are times when a teacher simply needs to stay on track. This does not mean that such ideas should be completely abandoned. Rather, teachers who effectively support creative ideas establish clear routines that accommodate situations when they determine that they need to stay on track with a lesson but still want to encourage and explore students' unexpected ideas. Examples of how this can be accomplished include: establishing a virtual or actual "idea dropbox" to

allow students to elaborate on or resubmit ideas; using a portion of the chalkboard as an "idea parking lot" for ideas that are not fully developed but can be revisited; and having students keep an idea book that includes an "idea garden" for new ideas and even an "idea grave yard" for ideas that have been put to rest in light of subsequent learning and insights.

13. *Teaching for creativity is more about "small wins" rather than radical curricular changes.* The life of a teacher is one that is marked by continual recommendations, pressures, and occasional mandates to adopt some new instructional approach, learning strategy, assessment technique, or curricular materials. Such changes often require teachers to make large (and sometimes quite radical) changes to their curriculum. Teachers may feel similar pressures when considering what it means for them to incorporate creativity into their classrooms. This can raise some daunting questions for teachers, including, "Do I somehow need to add creative activities into my lessons, and, if so, how can I possibly add yet another thing to an already overflowing plate of curricular responsibilities? Do I need to replace all my instructional units with a new creativity-based curriculum? Do I need to 'flip' my classroom and post my instructional lessons to *YouTube* so I have time to teach more creatively? Where will I get the time, training, and capacity to adopt such approaches and sustain them, when I'm also required to help my students meet externally mandated performance benchmarks?" Although it may be the case that more radical curricular changes can result in supporting students' creative competence, much can be gained by simply making slight changes to what one is already doing (Chapter 8). Teaching for and with creativity is often more about doing what one is already doing, only slightly better, rather than trying to do something completely different.

14. *Plan for creativity.* When it comes to supporting creativity in the classroom, much depends on how teachers plan their lessons. Lesson planning is a quintessential teaching behavior—learned early in preparation of teachers—and serves as a way to help organize a teacher's thinking, helps clarify what one intends to teach, and helps teachers imagine various possibilities for how a lesson might unfold. In a very real way, lesson planning is a generative creative activity that can, in turn, provide opportunities for creative expression and academic subject matter learning. How teachers approach their planning, therefore, plays a non-trivial role in whether and how creative expression will have an opportunity to manifest and be supported (see Chapter 8). If lesson planning has its basis in the assumption that the only way to provide a coherent, meaning-

ful learning experience is for teachers to somehow anticipate and eliminate all uncertainty from a lesson, then surprising turns in the curriculum will be viewed as signifiers of poor lesson planning rather than creative opportunities (see Chapter 4). When this happens, lesson planning becomes an overly prescriptive sequencing of events and results in the production of lesson plans that take on a life of their own—dictating to teachers a single, inflexible trajectory for a lesson. When lesson plans become moment-to-moment prescriptions, they serve to engineer away any alternative opportunities for new and meaningful learning to occur. Conversely, creative teachers approach their lesson planning with the recognition that it is a creative (rather than prescriptive) act. Creative teachers focus on developing a lesson plan that serves as a flexible structure that can accommodate unexpected curricular opportunities and, at the same time, serves as a thematic touchstone to return to if a lesson starts to drift too far off course. At its best, lesson planning is approached with possibility thinking (Craft, 2005), anticipates unexpected curricular moments, affords time in the lesson for the exploration of ideas, and blends flexibility with structure so that teachers have enough guidance and freedom to simultaneously support creative expression and academic subject matter learning.

15. *Teach and live creatively.* Teachers are powerful role models. One of the best ways to encourage students to approach learning and life creatively is to model creativity in the way we approach our own learning and lives (Chapter 8). This of course is easier said than done. One reason is that we can sometimes become so focused on our students' creativity that we sometimes forget about our own creativity. If teachers model the importance of approaching learning and life creatively, however, then their students likely will also learn the importance of creativity in learning and life. Teachers often do this modeling unconsciously. The good news is that teachers can also model such behaviors more consciously. Examples of some of the things that teachers can model on an everyday basis include: being willing to take intellectual risks, make mistakes, and learn from those mistakes; being open to new experiences—approaching unexpected learning moments with curiosity and a sense of possibility; recognizing that some of the most meaningful learning experiences emerge from unplanned and difficult to predict moments; approaching learning assignments, experiences, and tasks with a sense of "what if" instead of only what needs to be done, how it needs to be done, and when it needs to be done; being willing to try to do things in new ways, demonstrate persistence, admit to not knowing how to do things, discuss the challenges you have

faced and how you have overcome those challenges, and explain how and when you have adopted new ideas and approaches in order to learn new things; and demonstrating the habit of exploring unexpected ideas first, then evaluating the merit of those ideas in relation to the particular context of an academic discussion, assignment, or task.

I encourage teachers to frequently visit the above reminders and make lists of their own. I also encourage teachers to share their experiences incorporating creativity with others by starting study groups with like-minded colleagues, parents, and community members. Moreover, I encourage teachers to also share their experiences through self-study of their own efforts, discussing and reporting their insights at local and national educational conferences, through blogging, and reaching out to the creativity research community. I personally would be interested in hearing the experiences, questions, and comments of teachers who are approaching their teaching more creatively. I therefore encourage teachers to contact me directly (ron.beghetto@gmail.com).

RESOURCES FOR LEARNING MORE ABOUT CREATIVITY

Below are several resources where teachers can learn more about creativity so that they can be in a position to make their own unique and meaningful contributions to creative teaching and learning.

Creativity Related Books

- Beghetto, R. A. & Kaufman, J. C. (Eds.). (2010). *Nurturing creativity in the classroom.* New York, NY: Cambridge University Press.
- Fishkin, A. S., Cramond, B., & Olszewski-Kubilius, P. (Eds.). (1999). *Investigating creativity in youth.* Cresskill, NJ: Hampton Press.
- Gregerson, M., Kaufman, J. C., & Snyder, H. (Eds.). (2013). *Teaching creatively and teaching creativity.* New York, NY: Springer Science.
- Kaufman, J. C. & Sternberg, R. J. (Eds.). (2010). *Handbook of creativity.* New York, NY: Cambridge University Press.
- Runco, M. A. (2007). *Creativity theories and themes: Research, development and practice.* Burlington, MA: Elsevier Academic Press.
- Saracho, O. N. (Ed.). (2012). *Contemporary perspectives on research in creativity in early childhood education.* Charlotte, NC: Information Age Publishing.
- Sawyer, R. K. (2012). *Explaining creativity: The science of human innovation.* Oxford, UK: Oxford University Press.
- Sawyer, R. K. (Ed.). (2011). *Structure and improvisation in creative teaching.* New York, NY: Cambridge University Press.

- Tan, A. G. (Ed.). (2007). *Creativity: A handbook for teachers.* Singapore: World Scientific.

Creativity Related Journals

- *Creativity Research Journal,* Lawrence Erlbaum Associates, Inc.
- *Gifted Child Quarterly,* National Association for Gifted Children
- *High Ability Studies,* Routledge
- *Journal of Creative Behavior,* Creative Education Foundation, Inc.
- *International Journal of Creativity and Thinking Skills,* Korean Association for Thinking Development
- *Psychology of Aesthetics, Creativity, and the Arts,* American Psychological Association
- *Roeper Review,* Roeper School
- *Thinking Skills and Creativity,* Elsevier

Creativity Related Organizations

- American Creativity Association (www.aca.cloverpad.org)
- Center for Creative Learning (http://www.creativelearning.com)
- Creative Education Foundation (www.creativeeducationfoundation.org)
- Creative Problem Solving Group (http://www.cpsb.com)
- Society for the Psychology of Aesthetics, Creativity, and the Arts. Division 10 of the American Psychological Association (www.apa.org/divisions/div10)

REFERENCES

Akerson, V. L., Flick, L. B., & Lederman, N. G. (2000). The influence of primary children's ideas in science on teaching practices. *Journal of Research in Science Teaching, 37,* 363–385.

Aljughaiman, A. & Mowrer-Reynolds, E. (2005). Teachers' conceptions of creativity and creative students. *Journal of Creative Behavior, 39,* 17–34.

Alvarez, C. & Howard, A. (Producers). (2010, December). Stephen Sondheim: Finishing the hat. *Bookworm.* [Audio podcast]. Retrieved from http://www.kcrw.com/etc/programs/bw/bw101223stephen_sondheim_fin

Amabile, T. M. (1979). Effects of external evaluation on artistic creativity. *Journal of Personality and Social Psychology, 37,* 221–233.

Amabile, T. M. (1982). Children's artistic creativity: Detrimental effects of competition in a field setting. *Personality and Social Psychology Bulletin, 8,* 573–578.

Amabile, T. M. (1996). *Creativity in context: Update to the social psychology of creativity.* Boulder, CO: Westview.

Amabile, T. M., Conti, R., Coon, H., Lazenby, J., & Herron, M. (1996). Assessing the work environment for creativity. *The Academy of Management Journal, 39,* 1154–1184.

Amabile, T. M., DeJong, W., & Lepper, M. R. (1976). Effects of externally imposed deadlines on subsequent intrinsic motivation. *Journal of Personality and Social Psychology, 34,* 92–98.

Killing Ideas Softly? The Promise and Perils of Creativity in the Classroom, pages 149–161.

Copyright © 2013 by Information Age Publishing
149

Amabile, T. M., Goldfarb, P., & Brackfield, S. C. (1990). Social influences on creativity: evaluation, coaction, and surveillance. *Creativity Research Journal, 3,* 6–21.

Amabile, T. M., Hennessey, B. A., & Grossman, B. S. (1986). Social influences on creativity: The effects of contracted-for reward. *Journal of Personality and Social Psychology, 50,* 14–23.

Aoki, T. T. (2004). Spinning inspirited images. In W. F. Pinar & R. L. Irwin (Eds.), *Curriculum in a new key: The collected works of Ted T. Aoki* (pp. 413–425). Mahwah, NJ: Lawrence Erlbaum Associates.

Association of American Colleges and Universities (AACU). (2008). College learning for the new global century. Retrieved from http://www.aacu.org/advocacy/leap/documents/GlobalCentury_final.pdf

Baer. J. (2003). Impact of the core knowledge curriculum on creativity. *Creativity Research Journal, 15,* 297–300.

Baer, J. & Garrett, T. (2010). Teaching for creativity in an era of content standards and accountability. In R. A. Beghetto & J. C. Kaufman (Eds.), *Nurturing creativity in the classroom* (pp. 6–23). New York, NY: Cambridge University Press.

Baer, J. & Kaufman, J. C. (2005). Bridging generality and specificity: The amusement park theoretical (APT) model of creativity. *Roeper Review, 27,* 158–163.

Baillargeon, R., Needham, A., & DeVos, J. (1992). The development of young infants' intuitions about support. *Early Development Parenting, 1,* 69–78.

Bakhtin, M. (1981). *The dialogic imagination.* Austin, TX: University of Texas Press.

Baldwin, A. Y. (2010). Creativity: A look outside the box in classrooms. In R. A. Beghetto & J. C. Kaufman (Eds.), *Nurturing creativity in the classroom.* New York, NY: Cambridge University Press.

Ball, D. L. (1993). With an eye on the mathematical horizon: Dilemmas of teaching elementary school mathematics. *The Elementary School Journal, 93,* 373–397.

Bandura, A. (1997). *Self-efficacy: The exercise of control.* New York, NY: Freeman.

Baron, R. A. (1988). Negative effects of destructive criticism: Impact on conflict, self-efficacy, and task performance. *Journal of Applied Psychology, 73,* 199–207.

Barron, F. (1955). The disposition towards originality. *Journal of Abnormal Social Psychology, 51,* 478–485.

Bass, H. (2005). Mathematics, mathematicians, and mathematics education. *Bulletin of the American Mathematical Society, 42,* 417–430.

Beghetto, R. A. (2006). Creative self-efficacy: Correlates in middle and secondary students. *Creativity Research Journal, 18,* 447–457.

Beghetto, R. A. (2007a). Does creativity have a place in classroom discussions? Prospective teachers' response preferences. *Thinking Skills and Creativity, 2,* 1–9.

Beghetto, R. A. (2007b). Ideational code-switching: Walking the talk about supporting student creativity in the classroom. *Roeper Review, 29,* 265–270.

Beghetto, R. A. (2007c). Prospective teachers' beliefs about students' goal orientations: A carry-over effect of prior schooling experiences? *Social Psychology of Education, 10,* 171–191.

Beghetto, R. A. (2008). Prospective teachers' beliefs about imaginative thinking in K–12 schooling. *Thinking Skills and Creativity, 3,* 134–142.

Beghetto, R. A. (2009a). Correlates of intellectual risk taking in elementary school science. *Journal of Research in Science Teaching, 46,* 210–223.

Beghetto, R. A. (2009b). In search of the unexpected: Finding creativity in the micromoments of the classroom. *Psychology of Aesthetics, Creativity, and the Arts, 3,* 2–5.

Beghetto, R. A. (2010a). Creativity in the classroom. In J. C. Kaufman & R. J. Sternberg (Eds.), *Cambridge handbook of creativity.* New York, NY: Cambridge University Press.

Beghetto, R. A. (2010b). Prospective teachers' prior experiences with creativity suppression. *International Journal of Creativity and Problem Solving, 20,* 29–36.

Beghetto, R. A. (2011, August). *Creative mortification.* Paper presented at the 119th Annual Convention of the American Psychological Association, Washington, DC.

Beghetto, R. A. (in press). Creativity: Development and enhancement. To appear in J. A. Plucker & C. M. Callahan (Eds.), *Critical issues and practices in gifted education: What the research says* (2nd ed.). Waco, TX: Prufrock

Beghetto, R. A. (2013a). Expect the unexpected: Teaching for creativity in the micromoments. In M. Gregerson, J. C. Kaufman, & H. Snyder (Eds.), *Teaching creatively and teaching creativity* (pp. 133–148). New York, NY: Springer Science.

Beghetto, R. A. (2013b). Nurturing creativity in the micromoments of the classroom. In K. H. Kim, J. C. Kaufman, J. Baer, B. Sriramen, & L. Skidmore (Eds.), *Creatively gifted students are not like other gifted students: Research, theory, and practice* (pp. 3–15). The Netherlands: Sense Publishers.

Beghetto, R. A., & Baxter, J. (2012). Exploring student beliefs and understanding in elementary science and mathematics. *Journal of Research in Science Teaching, 49,* 942–960

Beghetto, R. A. & Kaufman, J. C. (2007). Toward a broader conception of creativity: A case for mini-c creativity. *Psychology of Aesthetics, Creativity, and the Arts, 1,* 73–79.

Beghetto, R. A. & Kaufman, J. C. (2009). Intellectual estuaries: Connecting learning and creativity in programs of advanced academics. *Journal of Advanced Academics, 20,* 296–324.

Beghetto, R. A. & Kaufman, J. C. (2010a). Broadening conceptions of creativity in the classroom. In R. A. Beghetto & J. C. Kaufman (Eds.), *Nurturing creativity in the classroom.* New York, NY: Cambridge University Press.

Beghetto, R. A. & Kaufman, J. C. (Eds.). (2010b). *Nurturing creativity in the classroom.* New York, NY: Cambridge University Press.

Beghetto, R. A. & Kaufman, J. C. (2011). Teaching for creativity with disciplined improvisation. In R. K. Sawyer (Ed.), *Structure and improvisation in creative teaching.* Cambridge: Cambridge University Press.

Beghetto, R. A., Kaufman, J. C., & Baxter, J. (2011). Answering the unexpected questions: Exploring the relationship between students' creative self-efficacy and teacher ratings of creativity. *Psychology of Aesthetics, Creativity and the Arts, 5,* 342–349.

Beghetto, R. A., Kaufman, J. C., Hegarty, B., Hammond, H., & Wilcox-Herzog, A. (2012). Cultivating creativity, play and leisure in early childhood education: A 4 C perspective. In O. N. Saracho & B. Spodek (Eds.), *Contemporary perspectives on creativity in early childhood education* (pp. 251–270). Charlotte, NC: Information Age Publishing.

Beghetto, R. A. & Plucker, J. A. (2006). The relationship among schooling, learning, and creativity: "All roads lead to creativity" or "You can't get there from here?" In J. C. Kaufman & J. Baer (Eds), *Creativity and reason in cognitive development* (pp. 316–332). Cambridge: Cambridge University Press.

Berliner, D. C. (2011). Narrowing curriculum, assessments, and conceptions of what it means to be smart in the U.S. schools: Creaticide by design. In D. Ambrose & R. J. Sternberg (Eds.), *How dogmatic beliefs harm creativity and higher-level thinking* (pp. 79–93). New York, NY: Routledge.

Berliner, P. F. (1994). *Thinking in jazz: The infinite art of improvisation.* Chicago, IL: University of Chicago Press.

Besemer, S. P. & Treffinger, D. J. (1981). Analysis of creative products: Review and synthesis. *Journal of Creative Behavior, 15,* 158–178.

Black, P. & Wiliam, D. (1998). Inside the black box: Raising standards through classroom 556 assessment. *Phi Delta Kappan, 80,* 139–148.

Blair, C. S. & Mumford, M. D. (2007). Errors in idea evaluation: Preference for the unoriginal? *Journal of Creative Behavior, 41,* 197–222.

Bonawitz, E., Shafto, P., Hyowon, G., Goodman, N. D., Spelke, E., & Schulz, L. (2010). The double-edged sword of pedagogy: Instruction limits spontaneous exploration and discovery. *Cognition.* Advance online publication. doi:10.1016/j.cognition.2010.10.001

Bonk, C. (2009, October). How does 'the worlds youngest teacher' use web technology? An interview with Adora Svitak. Retrieved from http://travelinedman. blogspot.com/2009/10/how-does-worlds-youngest-teacher-use.html

Borko, H. & Livingston, C. (1989). Cognition and improvisation: Differences in mathematics instruction by expert and novice teachers. *American Educational Research Journal, 26,* 473–498.

Borko, H. & Putnam, R. (1996). Learning to teach. In R. Calfee & D. Berliner (Eds.), *Handbook of educational psychology* (pp. 69–87). New York, NY: Macmillan.

Bronson, P. O. & Merryman, A. (2010, July 19). The creativity crisis. *Newsweek,* pp. 44–50.

Brown A. L. & Palincsar, A. S. (1989). Guided cooperative learning and individual knowledge acquisition. In L. Resnick (Ed.), *Knowing, learning, and instruction: Essays in honor of Robert Glaser* (pp. 393–451). Hillsdale, NJ: Erlbaum

Buchsbaum, D., Gopnik, A., Griffiths, T. L., & Shafto, P. (2010). Children's imitation of causal action sequences is influenced by statistical and pedagogical evidence. *Cognition, 120*(3), 331–340. doi:10.1016/j.cognition.2010.12.001

Byrnes, J. P. (1998). *The nature and development of decision-making: A self-regulation model.* Hillsdale, NJ: Erlbaum.

Calderhead, J. & Robson, M. (1991). Images of teaching: Student teachers' early conceptions of classroom practice. *Teaching and Teacher Education, 7,* 1–8.

Callahan, C. M. & Miller, E. M. (2005). A child-responsive model of giftedness. In R. J. Sternberg & J. E. Davidson (Eds.), *Conceptions of giftedness* (2nd ed., pp. 38–50). Cambridge: Cambridge University Press.

Cazden, C. B. (2001). *Classroom discourse: The language of teaching and learning* (2nd ed.). Portsmouth, NH: Heinemann.

Cianci, A. M., Klein, H. J., & Seijts, G. H. (2010). The effect of negative feedback on tension and subsequent performance: The main and interactive effects of goal content and conscientiousness. *Journal of Applied Psychology, 4*, 618–630.

Cimpian, A., Arce, H. C., Markman, E. M., & Dweck, C. S. (2007). Subtle linguistic cues affect children's motivation. *Psychological Science, 18*, 314–316.

Clark, C. M. & Yinger, R. J. (1977). Research on teacher thinking. *Curriculum Inquiry, 7*, 279–304.

Claxton, A. F., Pannells, T. C., & Rhoads, P. A. (2005). Developmental trends in the creativity of school-age children. *Creativity Research Journal, 17*, 327–335.

Claxton, G. (2008). *What's the point of school? Rediscovering the heart of education.* Oxford, UK: Oneworld publications.

Clifford, M. M. (1991). Risk taking: Theoretical, empirical, and educational considerations. *Educational Psychologist, 26*, 263–297.

Clifford, M. M. & Chou, F. (1991). Effects of payoff and task context on academic risk taking. *Journal of Educational Psychology, 83*, 499–507.

Cohen, L. M. (1989). A continuum of adaptive creative behaviors. *Creativity Research Journal, 2*, 169–183.

Cole, D. (2004). The Chinese room argument. In E. N. Zalta (Ed.), The Stanford encyclopedia of philosophy (fall 2004 ed.). Retrieved from http://plato.stanford.edu/archives/fall2012/entries/chinese-room/

Collins, M. A. & Amabile, T. M. (1999). Motivation and creativity. In R. J. Sternberg (Ed.), *Handbook of creativity* (pp. 297–312). Cambridge: Cambridge University Press.

Craft, A. (2005). *Creativity in schools: Tensions and dilemmas.* New York, NY: Routledge.

Craft, A. (2007). Possibility thinking in the early years and primary classroom. In A. G. Tan (Ed.), *Creativity: A handbook for teachers* (pp. 231–250). Singapore: World Scientific.

Craft, A. (2010). Possibility thinking and wise creativity: Educational future in England? In R. A. Beghetto & J. C. Kaufman (Eds.), *Nurturing creativity in the classroom* (pp. 289–312). New York, NY: Cambridge University Press.

Craft, A. (2011). *Creativity and education futures: Learning in a digital age.* England: Trentham Books.

Cubberley, E. P. (1916). *Public school administration: A statement of the fundamental principles underlying the organization and administration of public education.* Boston, MA: Houghton Mifflin Company.

Darling-Hammond, L. & Rustique-Forrester, E. (2005). The consequences of student testing for teaching and teacher quality. *Yearbook of the National Society for the Study of Education, 104*, 289–319.

Davis, A. & Stratton, A. R. (2010). *Inward light: A drama in four acts.* Whitefish, MT: Kessinger Publishing. [Original work published 1919]

Davidson, J. E. & Sternberg, R. (1998). Smart problem solving: How metacognition helps. In D. J. Hacker, A. C. Graesser, & J. Dunlosky (Eds.), *Metacognition in educational theory and practice* (pp. 47–69). Mahwah, NJ: Lawrence Erlbaum Associates.

de Groot, A. D. (1965). *Thought and choice in chess.* The Netherlands: Mouton.

DeMunn, N. W. & Snow, F. B. (Eds.). (1865). Discouraging attempts to sing. *The Rhode Island Schoolmaster, 11*, 88–89.

Dewey, J. (1897). My pedagogic creed. *School Journal, 54,* 77–80.

Dewey, J. (2005). *Art as experience.* New York, NY: Perigee Books. (Original work published 1934)

Dewey, J. (2007). *The school and society.* New York, NY: Cosimo. (Original work published 1899)

Dickens, C. (2008). *Hard times.* Oxford: Oxford University Press.

Donovan, S. M. & Bransford, J. D. (Eds.). (2005). *How students learn: History, mathematics, and science in the classroom.* Washington, DC: The National Academies Press.

Dunning, D., Health, C., & Suls, J. M. (2004). Flawed self-assesment: Implications for health, education, and the workplace. *Psychological Science in the Public Interest, 5,* 69–106.

Dweck, C. S. (2000). *Self-theories: Their role in motivation, personality, and development.* Philadelphia, PA: Psychology Press.

Eberle, B. (1996). *SCAMPER: Games for imagination development.* Waco, TX: Prufrock Press.

Egan, K. & Gajdamaschko, N. (2003). Some cognitive tools of literacy. In A. Kozulin, B. Gindis, V. S. Ageyev, & S. M. Miller (Eds.), *Vygotsky's educational theory in cultural context* (pp. 83–98). Cambridge, UK: Cambridge University Press.

Eisenberger, R. & Cameron, J. (1998). Reward, intrinsic interest, and creativity: New findings. *American Psychologist, 53,* 676–679.

Eisenberger, R. & Shanock, L. (2003). Rewards, intrinsic motivation, and creativity: A case study of conceptual and methodological isolation. *Creativity Research Journal, 15,* 121–130.

Eisner, E. W. (2002). *The arts and the creation of mind.* New Haven, CT: Yale University Press.

Ericsson, K. A. (Ed.). (1996). *The road to expert performance: empirical evidence from the arts and sciences, sports, and games.* Mahwah, NJ: Erlbaum.

Fairweather, E. & Cramond, B. (2010). Infusing creativity and critical thinking into the curriculum together. In R. A. Beghetto & J. C. Kaufman (Eds.), *Nurturing creativity in the classroom* (pp. 113–141). New York, NY: Cambridge University Press.

Feist, G. J. (1998). A meta-analysis of personality in scientific and artistic creativity. *Personality and Social Psychology Review, 2,* 290–309.

Feldhusen, J. F. & Goh, B. E. (1995). Assessing and accessing creativity: An integrative review of theory, research, and development. *Creativity Research Journal, 8,* 231–248.

Ferrari, A., Cachia, R., & Punie, Y. (2009). *Innovation and creativity in education and training in the EU member states: Fostering creative learning and supporting innovative teaching. Literature review on Innovation and creativity in E&T in the EU member states (ICEAC).* Luxembourg: Office for Official Publications of the European Communities.

Fitch, G. H. (1912). *Modern English books of power.* New York, NY: Barse & Hopkins.

Flavell, J. (1979). Metacognition and cognitive monitoring: A new area of cognitive-developmental inquiry. *American Psychologist, 34,* 906–911.

Florida, R. (2004). *The rise of the creative class: And how it's transforming work, leisure, community and everyday life.* New York, NY: Basic Books.

Ford, D. Y. & Grantham, T. C. (2003). Providing access for culturally diverse gifted students: From deficit to dynamic thinking. *Theory into Practice, 42,* 217–225.

Fried, R. L. (2005). *The game of school: Why we all play it, how it hurts kids, and what it will take to change it.* San Francisco, CA: Jossey-Bass.

Gerrard, L. E., Poteat, G. M., & Ironsmith, M. (1996). Promoting children's creativity: Effects of competition, self-esteem, and immunization. *Creativity Research Journal, 9,* 339–346.

Getzels, J. W. & Csikszentmihalyi, M. (1976). *The creative vision: A longitudinal study of problem finding in art.* New York, NY: Wiley.

Goodlad, J. L. (2004). *A place called school: Prospects for the future.* New York, NY: Mc-Grall-Hill.

Greene, M. (1995). *Releasing the imagination: Essays on education, the arts, and social change.* San Francisco, CA: Jossey-Bass.

Grigorenko, E. L., Jarvin, L., Tan, M., & Sternberg, R. J. (2008). Something new in the garden: Assessing creativity in academic domains. *Psychology Science Quarterly, 50,* 295–307.

Guilford, J. P. (1950). Creativity. *American Psychologist, 5,* 444–454.

Guilford, J. P. (1959). Traits of creativity. In H. H. Anderson (Ed.), *Creativity and its cultivation* (pp. 142–161). New York, NY: Harpers.

Halpern, C., Close, D., & Johnson, K. (1994). *Truth in comedy: The manual of improvisation.* Colorado Springs, CO: Meriwether Publishing.

Hannah, C. L. & Abate, R. J. (Producers). (1995). Classroom insights II [VHS]. Boston, MA: Allyn & Bacon.

Harvard-Smithsonian Center for Astrophysics (HSCA). (Producer). (2000). *Private universe project in mathematics.* Retrieved from http://www.learner.org/resources/series120.html

Hatano, G. (1993). Time to merge Vygotskian and constructivist conceptions of knowledge acquisition. In E. A. Forman, N. Minick, & C. A. Stone (Eds.), *Contexts for learning: Sociocultural dynamics in children's development* (pp. 153–166). New York, NY: Oxford University Press.

Hennessey, B. A. (2010a). Intrinsic motivation and creativity in the classroom: Have we come full circle? In R. A. Beghetto & J. C. Kaufman (Eds.), *Nurturing creativity in the classroom* (pp. 329–361). New York, NY: Cambridge University Press.

Hennessey, B. A. (2010b). The creativity-motivation connection. In J. C. Kaufman & R. J. Sternberg (Eds.), *The Cambridge handbook of creativity* (pp. 329–361). New York, NY: Cambridge University Press.

Heinrich, C. (2000). *Monet.* Cologne, Germany: Taschen.

Hong, E. & Milgram, R. M. (2007). *Preventing talent loss.* New York, NY: Routledge.

hooks, b. (1994). *Teaching to transgress: Education as the practice of freedom.* New York, NY: Routledge.

Housner, L. D. & Griffey, D. C. (1985). Teacher cognition: Differences in planning and interactive decision making between experienced and inexperienced teachers. *Research Quarterly for Exercise and Sport, 56,* 45–53.

Hunter, S. T., Bedell, K. E., & Mumford, M. D. (2007). Climate for creativity: A quantitative review. *Creativity Research Journal, 19,* 69–90.

Ingersoll, R. M. (2003). *Who controls teachers' work? Power and accountability in America's schools.* Cambridge, MA: Harvard University Press.

Isaksen, S. G. & Treffinger, D. J. (2004). Celebrating 50 years of reflective practice: Versions of creative problem solving. *Journal of Creative Behavior, 38,* 75–101.

Jeffrey, B. & Craft, A. (2004). Teaching creatively and teaching for creativity: Distinctions and relationships. *Educational Studies, 30,* 77–87.

Kamii, C. (2000). *Double-column addition: A teacher uses Piaget's theory* [VHS Tape]. New York: Teachers College.

Karpovsky, A. (Director). (2009). *Trust us this is all made up.* New York, NY: New Video Group.

Kaufman, J. C., & Baer, J. (Eds). (2005). *Creativity across domains: Faces of the muse.* Mahwah, NJ: Lawrence Erlbaum.

Kaufman, J. C., Baer, J., & Cole, J. C. (2009). Expertise, domains, and the consensual assessment technique. *Journal of Creative Behavior, 43,* 223–233.

Kaufman, J. C., Baer, J., Cole, J. C., & Sexton, J. D. (2008). A comparison of expert and nonexpert raters using the Consensual Assessment Technique. *Creativity Research Journal, 20,* 171–178.

Kaufman, J. C. & Beghetto, R. A. (2009). Beyond big and little: The four C model of creativity. *Review of General Psychology, 13,* 1–12.

Kaufman, J. C. & Beghetto, R. A. (in press). In praise of Clark Kent: Creative metacognition and the importance of teaching kids when (not) to be creative. *Roeper Review.*

Kaufman, J. C., Plucker, J. A., & Baer, J. (2008). *Essentials of creativity assessment.* New York, NY: Wiley.

Keller, C. M. & Keller, J. D. (1996). *Cognition and tool use: The blacksmith at work.* New York, NY: Cambridge University Press

Kennedy, M. (2005). *Inside teaching: How classroom life undermines reform.* Cambridge, MA: Harvard University Press.

Kim, K. H. (2011). The creativity crisis: The decrease in creative thinking scores on the Torrance Tests of Creative Thinking. *Creativity Research Journal, 23,* 285–295.

Kozbelt, A. (2007). A quantitative analysis of Beethoven as self-critic: Implications for psychological theories of musical creativity. *Psychology of Music, 35,* 147–172.

Kozbelt, A., Beghetto, R. A., & Runco, M. A. (2010). Theories of creativity. In J. C. Kaufman & R. J. Sternberg (Eds.), *Handbook of creativity* (pp. 20–47). Cambridge: Cambridge University Press.

Kozulin, A. (2003). Psychological tools and mediated learning. In A.Kozulin, B. Gindis, V. S. Ageyev, & S. M. Miller (Eds.), *Vygotsky's educational theory in cultural context* (pp. 15–38). Cambridge, UK: Cambridge University Press.

Kruglanski, A. W., Friedman, I., & Zeevi, G. (1971). The effects of extrinsic incentive on some qualitative aspects of task performance. *Journal of Personality, 39,* 606–617.

Lampert, M. (1990). When the problem is not the question and the solution is not the answer: Mathematical knowing and teaching. *American Educational Research Journal, 27,* 29–63.

Lewis, M. & Sullivan, M. W. (2005). The development of self-conscious emotion. In A. J. Elliot & C. S. Dweck (Eds.), *Handbook of competence and motivation* (pp. 185–201). New York, NY: Guilford Press.

Lilly, F. R. & Bramwell-Rejskind, G. (2004). The dynamics of creative teaching. *Journal of Creative Behavior, 38,* 102–124.

Lockhart, B. (2012). A specific and fleeting moment of time. Retrieved from http://www.bill.lockharts.com/blog/a-specific-and-fleeting-moment-of-time/

Lortie, D. (1975). *Schoolteacher: A sociological study.* Chicago, IL: University of Chicago Press.

Mack, A. & Rock, I. (1998). *Inattentional blindness.* Cambridge, MA: MIT press.

Maehr, M. L. & Midgley, C. (1996). *Transforming school culture.* Boulder, CO: Westview Press.

Malloy, E. (Director). (2009). *The White Stripes under great white northern lights* [Motion picture]. Los Angeles, CA: Three Foot Giant.

Malmberg, L. E. (2006). Goal orientation and teacher motivation among teacher applicants and student teachers. *Teaching and Teacher Education, 22,* 58–76.

Maltzman, I. (1960). On the training of originality. *Psychological review, 67,* 229–242.

Marland, S. P. (1972). *Education of the gifted and talented: Report to the Congress of the United States by the U.S. Commissioner of Education.* Washington, DC: Department of Health, Education and Welfare.

Matusov, E. (2009). *Journey into dialogic pedagogy.* Hauppauge, NY: Nova Publishers.

McNeil, L. M. (2000). *Contradictions of school reform: Educational costs of standardized testing.* New York, NY: Routledge.

Mehan, H. (1979). *Learning lessons: Social organization in the classroom.* Cambridge, MA: Harvard University Press.

Mertler, C. A. (2001). Designing scoring rubrics for your classroom. *Practical Assessment, Research, and Evaluation, 7*(25). Retrieved from http://pareonline.net/getvn.asp?v=7&n=25

Midgley, C. (Ed.) (2002). *Goals, goal structures, and patterns of adaptive learning.* Mahwah, NJ: Erlbaum.

Mumford, M. D., Blair, C. S., & Marcy, R. T. (2006). Alternative knowledge structures in creative thought. In J. C. Kaufman & J. Bear (Eds.), *Creativity and reason in cognitive development* (pp. 117–136). Cambridge, UK: Cambridge University Press.

Nathan, M. J. & Knuth, E. J. (2003). A study of whole classroom mathematical discourse and teacher change. *Cognition and Instruction, 21,* 175–207.

National Research Council (NRC). (2000). *How people learn: Brain, mind, experience, and school.* Washington, DC: National Academies Press.

Needham, A. & Baillargeon, R. (1993). Intuitions about support in 4 1/2 month-old-infants. *Cognition, 47*(2), 121–148.

Neisser, U. (1979). The control of information pickup in selective looking. In A. D. Pick (Ed.), *Perception and its development: A tribute to Eleanor J. Gibson* (pp. 201–219). Hillsdale, NJ: Erlbaum.

Nickerson, R. S. (1999). Enhancing creativity. In R. J. Sternberg (Ed.), *Handbook of human creativity* (pp. 392–430). New York, NY: Cambridge University Press.

Niu, W. & Zhou, Z. (2010). Creativity in mathematics teaching: A Chinese perspective. In R. A. Beghetto & J. C. Kaufman (Eds.), *Nurturing creativity in the classroom* (pp. 270–288). New York, NY: Cambridge University Press.

O'Hara, L.A., & Sternberg, R. J. (2001). It doesn't hurt to ask: Effects of instructions to be creative, practical or analytical on essay-writing performance and their interaction with students' thinking styles. *Creativity Research Journal, 13,* 197–210.

Organisation for Economic Co-operation and Development (OECD). (2008). *Innovating to learn, learning to innovate.* Paris, France: Author.

Orenstein, P. (2011). How to unleash your creativity. Retrieved from http://www.oprah.com/spirit/How-to-Unleash-Your-Creativity

Pajares, M. F. (1992). Teachers' beliefs and educational research: Cleaning up a messing construct. *Review of Educational Research, 62,* 307–332.

Paley, V. G. (2007). HER Classic: On listening to what children say. *Harvard Educational Review, 77,* 152–163.

Palincsar, A. S. & Brown, A. L. (1984). Reciprocal teaching of comprehension-fostering and comprehension-monitoring activities. *Cognition and Instruction, 1,* 117–175.

Palincsar, A. S. & Brown A. L. (1989). Classroom dialogues to promote self-regulated comprehension. In J. Brophy (Ed.), *Advances in research on teaching* (pp. 25–72). Greenwich, CT: JAI

Partnership for 21st Century Schools (P21). (2011). *Framework for 21st century learning.* Retrieved from: http://www.p21.org/overview/skills-framework

Piirto, J. (2004). *Understanding creativity.* Scottsdale, AZ: Great Potential Press.

Pintrich, P. R., Wolters, C., & Baxter, G. (2000). Assessing metacognition and self-regulated learning. In G. Schraw & J. Impara (Eds.), *Issues in the measurement of metacognition* (pp. 43–97). Lincoln NE: Buros Institute of Mental Measurements.

Plucker, J. A. & Beghetto, R. A. (2004). Why creativity is domain general, why it looks domain specific, and why the distinction does not matter. In R. J. Sternberg, E. L. Grigorenko, & J. L. Singer (Eds.), *Creativity: From potential to realization* (pp. 153–167). Washington, DC: American Psychological Association.

Plucker, J., Beghetto, R. A., & Dow, G. (2004). Why isn't creativity more important to educational psychologists? Potential, pitfalls, and future directions in creativity research. *Educational Psychologist, 39,* 83–96.

Plucker, J. A. & Dow, G. T. (2010). Attitude change as the precursor to creativity enhancement. In R. A. Beghetto & J. C. Kaufman (Eds.), *Nurturing creativity in the classroom* (pp. 362–379). New York, NY: Cambridge University Press.

Plucker, J. A. & Makel, M. C. (2010). Assessment of creativity. In J. C. Kaufman & R. J. Sternberg (Eds.), *Handbook of creativity* (pp. 48–73). New York, NY: Cambridge University Press.

Reeve, J. (2009). Why teachers adopt a controlling motivating style toward students and how they can become more autonomy supportive. *Educational Psychologist, 44,* 159–175.

Rhodes, M. (1961). An analysis of creativity. *Phi Delta Kappan, 42,* 305–310.

Richards, R. (2007). Everyday creativity: Our hidden potential. In R. Richards (Ed.), *Everyday creativity and new views of human nature* (pp. 25–54). Washington, DC: American Psychological Association.

Richardson, V. (2003). Preservice teachers' beliefs. In J. Raths & A. C. McAninch (Eds.), *Teacher beliefs and classroom performance: The impact of teacher education* (pp. 1–22). Greenwich, CT: Information Age Publishing.

Ross, A. (1982, October). Notes. *London Magazine, 22,* 3–6.

Runco, M. A. (1996). Personal creativity: Definition and developmental issues. *New Directions in Child Development, 72,* 3–30.

Runco, M. A. (2003). Creativity, cognition, and their educational implications. In J. C. Houtz (Ed.), *The educational psychology of creativity* (pp. 25–56). Cresskill, NJ: Hampton Press.

Runco, M. A. (2007). *Creativity. Theories and themes: Research, development, and practice.* Burlington, MA: Elsevier Academic Press.

Runco, M. A. & Charles, R. E. (1993). Judgments of originality and appropriateness as predictors of creativity. *Personality and Individual Differences, 15,* 537–546.

Ryan, R. M. & Deci, E. L. (2000). Intrinsic and extrinsic motivations: Classic definitions and new directions. *Contemporary Educational Psychology, 25,* 54–67.

Ryan, R. M. & Deci, E. L. (2006). Self-regulation and the problem of human autonomy: Does psychology need choice, self-determination, and will? *Journal of Personality, 74,* 1557–1586.

Sabochik, K. (2010). *Changing the equation in STEM education.* Retreived from http://www.whitehouse.gov/blog/2010/09/16/changing-equation-stem-education

Saeta, E. (1997, September). A MELUS interview: Ana Castillo. [Interview]. Retrieved from http://business.highbeam.com/4352/article-1G1-20441304/melus-interview-ana-castillo

Sawyer, R. K. (2004). Creative teaching: Collaborative discussion as disciplined improvisation. *Educational Researcher, 33,* 12–20.

Sawyer, R. K. (2010). Learning for creativity. In R. A. Beghetto & J. C. Kaufman (Eds.), *Nurturing creativity in the classroom* (pp. 172–190). New York, NY: Cambridge University Press.

Sawyer, R. K. (Ed.). (2011). *Structure and improvisation in creative teaching.* New York, NY: Cambridge University Press.

Sawyer, R. K. (2012). *Explaining creativity: The science of human innovation* (2nd ed.). New York, NY: Oxford University Press.

Schneps, M. H. & Sadler, P. M. (1987). *A private universe* [Video]. Cambridge, MA: Harvard Smithsonian Center for Astrophysics.

Schrade, L. (1946). Bach: Conflict between the sacred and the secular. *Journal of the History of Ideas, 7,* 151–194.

Schuh, K. L. (2003). Knowledge construction in the learner-centered classroom. *Journal of Educational Psychology, 95,* 426–442.

Scott, G., Leritz, L. E., & Mumford, M. D. (2004). The effectiveness of creativity training: A quantitative review. *Creativity Research Journal, 16,* 361–388.

Shepard, L. A. (2001). The role of classroom assessment in teaching and learning. In V. Richardson (Ed.), *The handbook of research on teaching* (4th ed.). Washington, DC: American Educational Research Association.

Simons, D. J. & Chabris, C. F. (1999). Gorillas in our midst: Sustained inattentional blindness for dynamic events. *Perception, 28,* 1059–1074.

Simonton, D. K. (2003). Creativity as variation and selection: Some critical constraints. In M. A. Runco (Ed.), *Critical creative processes* (pp. 3–18). Cresskill, NJ: Hampton Press.

Simonton, D. K. (2009). Varieties of (scientific) creativity: A hierarchical model of domain-specific disposition, development, and achievement. *Perspectives on Psychological Science, 4,* 441–452.

Simonton, D. K. (2010). Creativity in highly eminent individuals. In J. C. Kaufman & R. J. Sternberg (Eds.). *The Cambridge handbook of creativity* (pp. 174–188). New York, NY: Cambridge University Press.

Sirotnik, K. A. (1983). What you see is what you get: Consistency, persistency, and mediocrity in classrooms. *Harvard Educational Review, 53,* 16–31.

Smith, J. K. & Smith, L. F. (2010). Educational creativity. In J. C. Kaufman & R. J. Sternberg (Eds.), *The Cambridge handbook of creativity* (pp. 250–264). New York, NY: Cambridge University Press.

Stein, M. I. (1953). Creativity and culture. *The Journal of Psychology, 36,* 311–322.

Steinman, H. (2010, April). The phoenix and the French laundry. *Wine Spectator.*

Sternberg, R. J. (2010). Teaching for creativity. In R. A. Beghetto & J. C. Kaufman (Eds.), *Nurturing creativity in the classroom* (pp. 394–414). New York, NY: Cambridge University Press

Sternberg, R. J. & Kaufman, J. C. (2010). Constraints on creativity: Obvious and not so obvious. In J. C. Kaufman & R. J. Sternberg (Eds.), *The Cambridge handbook of creativity* (pp. 467–482). New York, NY: Cambridge University Press.

Sternberg, R. J., Kaufman, J. C., & Pretz, J. E. (2002). *The creativity conundrum.* Philadelphia, PA: Psychology Press.

Sternberg, R. J. & Lubart, T. I. (1995). *Defying the crowd: Cultivating creativity in a culture of conformity.* New York, NY: Free Press.

Stokes, P. D. (2001). Variability, constraints, and creativity: Shedding light on Claude Monet. *American Psychologist, 56,* 355–359.

Tierney, P., & Farmer, S. M. (2002). Creative self-efficacy: Its potential antecedents and relationship to creative performance. *Academy of Management Journal, 45,* 1137–1148.

Tighe, E., Picariello, M. L., & Amabile, T. M. (2003). Environmental influences on motivation and creativity in the classroom. In J. C. Houtz (Ed.), *The educational psychology of creativity* (pp. 199–222). Cresskill, NJ: Hampton Press

Tobias, S. & Duffy, T. M. (Eds.). (2009). *Constructivist theory applied to instruction: Success or failure?* New York, NY: Taylor & Francis.

Torrance, E. P. (1959). Current research on the nature of creative talent. Journal of *Counseling Psychology, 6,* 309–316.

Torrance, E. P. (1966). *Torrance tests of creative thinking: Norms technical manual.* Princeton, NJ: Personnel.

Torrance, E. P. (1968). A longitudinal examination of the fourth grade slump in creativity. *Gifted Child Quarterly, 12,* 195–199.

Torrance, E. P. (1970). *Encouraging creativity in the classroom.* Dubuque, IA: William C. Brown Company.

Torrance, E. P. & Gupta, R. K. (1964). *Programmed experiences in creative thinking. Final report on Title VII Project to the U.S. Office of Education.* Minneapolis, MN: University of Minnesota.

Tracy, J. L. & Robins, R. W. (2004). Putting the self into self-conscious emotions: A theoretical model. *Psychological Inquiry, 15,* 103–125.

Tracy, J. L. & Robins, R. W. (2006). Appraisal antecedents of shame and guilt: Support for a theoretical model. *Personality and Social Psychology Bulletin, 32,* 1339–1351.

U.S. Department of Education (USDE). (1993). *National excellence: A case for developing America's talent.* Washington, DC: Author.

van Zee, E. H., Iwasyk, M., Kurose, A., Simpson, D., & Wild, J. (2001). Student and teacher questioning during conversations about science. *Journal of Research in Science Teaching, 38,* 159–190.

Vygotsky, L. S. (2004). Imagination and creativity in childhood. M. E. Sharpe, Inc. (Trans.). *Journal of Russian and East European Psychology, 42,* 7–97. (Original work published 1967)

Ward, T. B. (2008). The role of domain knowledge in creative generation. *Learning and Individual Differences, 18,* 363–366.

Warnock, M. (1978). *Imagination.* Berkeley, CA: University of California Press.

Webster, A., Campbell, C., & Jane, B. (2006). Enhancing the creative process for learning in primary technology education. *International Journal of Technology & Design Education, 16,* 221–235.

Weick, K. (1984). Small wins: Redefining the scale of social problems. *American Psychologist, 39,* 40–49.

Wells, G. & Claxton, G. (Eds.). (2002). *Learning for life in the 21st century.* Malden, MA: Blackwell.

Wheatley, M. J. (2007). *Finding our way: Leadership for an uncertain time.* San Francisco, CA: Berret-Kohler Publishers.

ABOUT THE AUTHOR

Dr. Beghetto is an Associate Professor of Educational Psychology in the Neag School of Education at the University of Connecticut.

Prior to joining the faculty at UConn, Dr. Beghetto served as the College of Education's Associate Dean for Academic Affairs and Associate Professor of Education Studies at the University of Oregon. He earned his Ph.D. in Educational Psychology from Indiana University (with an emphasis in Learning, Cognition and Instruction).

His research focuses on creativity in educational settings – examining how teacher and student creativity is sometimes (inadvertently) suppressed and how it can be incorporated in the everyday classroom. Dr. Beghetto has extensive experience working with practicing and prospective teachers in an effort to help them develop new and transformative possibilities for classroom teaching, learning, and assessment in K-12 and higher education settings. He has published numerous scholarly articles and book chapters on classroom creativity and teacher development.

Dr. Beghetto is the Editor-in-Chief for the Journal of Creative Behavior and serves as an associate editor for the International Journal of Creativity and Problem Solving. He also serves on the editorial boards of Psychology of Aesthetics, Creativity and the Arts; Journal of Educational Research; Gifted Child Quarterly, and Creativity: Theories, Research, and Applications.

Dr. Beghetto is a Fellow of the American Psychological Association and the Society for the Psychology of Aesthetics, Creativity and the Arts (Div. 10,

Killing Ideas Softly? The Promise and Perils of Creativity in the Classroom, page 163–164.

APA). He is the 2008 recipient of Daniel E. Berlyne Award from Division 10 of the American Psychological Association for outstanding research by an early career scholar. Dr. Beghetto has also received numerous awards for excellence in teaching. In Spring 2006 he received the University of Oregon 's highest teaching award for early career faculty (Ersted Crystal Apple Award).

Made in the USA
Las Vegas, NV
14 January 2021